AMBRA | V

Book series of the University of Applied Arts Vienna
Edited by Gerald Bast, President

edition: 'ʌngewʌndtə

THOUGHT MACHINES

THE MANUAL

to an international exhibition

AMBRA | V

INDEX

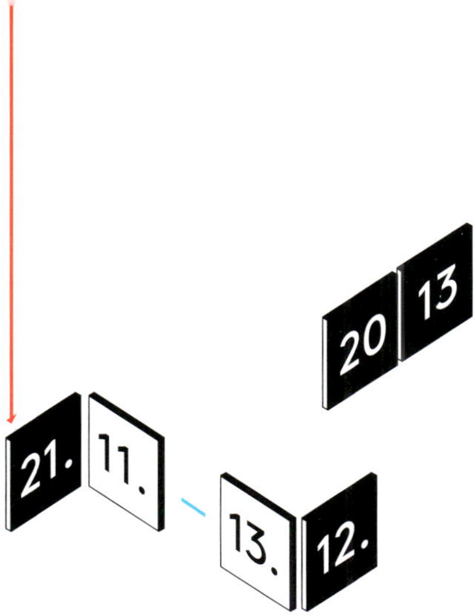

Exhibition Center Heiligenkreuzerhof
University of Applied Arts Vienna

HU Hungarian University of Fine Arts
BUDAPEST

SK Academy of Fine Arts and Design
BRATISLAVA

DE Academy of Visual Arts
LEIPZIG

GB Royal College of Art
LONDON

AT University of Applied Arts
VIENNA

PREFACE

AT **GERALD BAST**

President,
University of Applied Arts Vienna

Thinking machines are usually seen as highly sophisticated technical tools that can be run by human thoughts. But how about the thoughts themselves? What affects our way of thinking? Thoughts, after all, are the preconditions of all artwork.

The artists involved in this international project open up the field of perception toward the conditions under which thoughts are produced. They want to draw attention to the fact that the tools they use in producing art shape their thoughts and thereby affect their artwork – not only in terms of technique and superficial aestheticism, but even more in terms of meaning. Yes, art is very much about producing meaning and about demonstrating and amplifying values. The aesthetics of meaning are what makes art touching and thus influential to individuals and societies.

We are all influenced by the environment surrounding us – and tools are a main factor of environments. Of course we all know that it makes a great difference whether you travel on foot or by motorcycle, balloon or plane. Not only does the tool used to make the trip determine the route and the speed of your journey: it also shapes your mind very differently in each case.

Here, in focusing on the role of artistic tools, you are invited to set off on a journey toward discovering – or at least getting an idea of – how much they shape art. Along the way you may come to view the artworks, and also their meanings, as further stations on ______________________

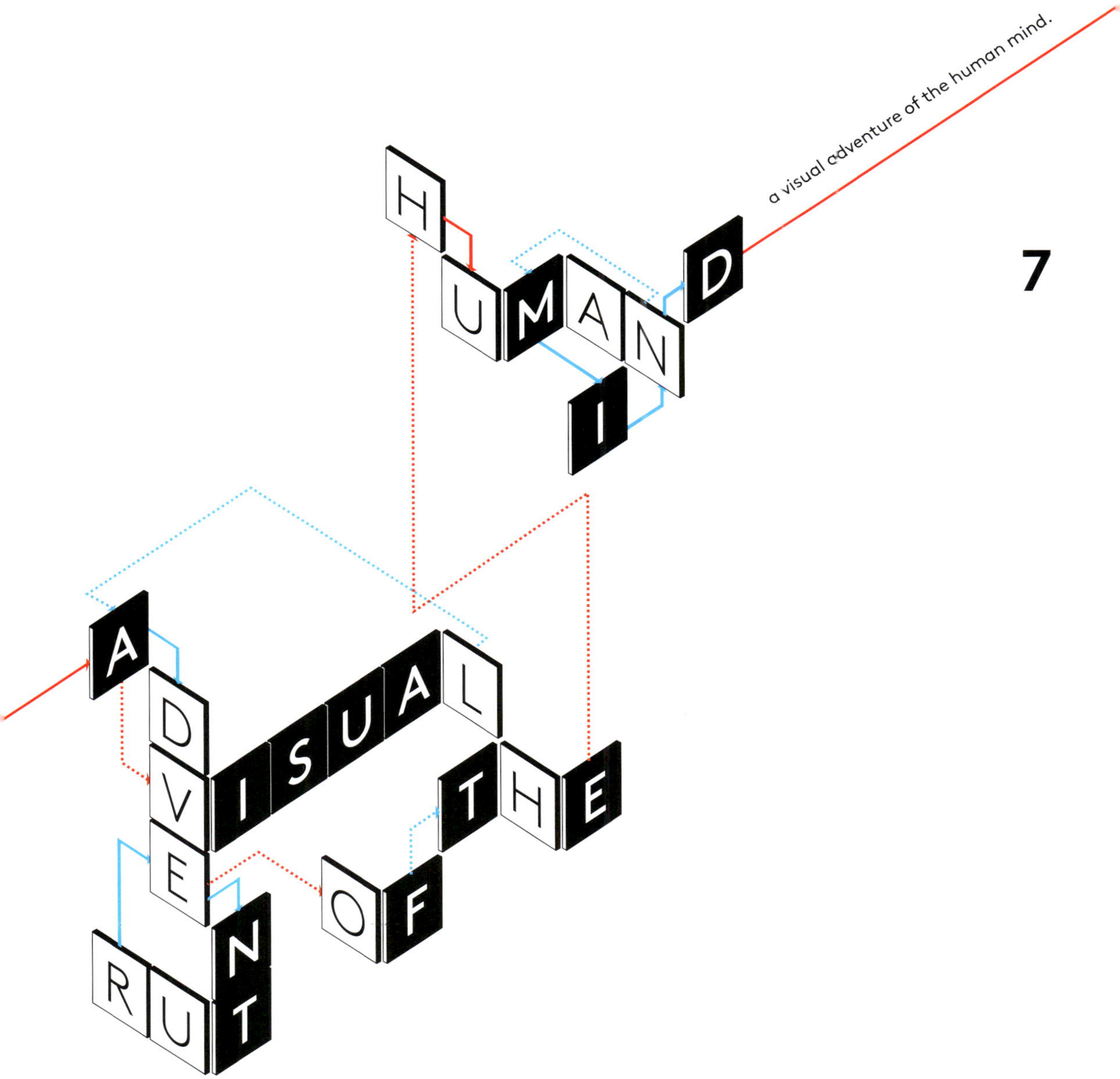
a visual adventure of the human mind.
HUMAN MIND
A VISUAL ADVENTURE OF THE

INTRO-DUCTION

AT JAN SVENUNGSSON

Professor, Head of the Department for Graphics and Printmaking, University of Applied Arts Vienna

We artists use tools to make our work. Pencils and brushes, computers and printing presses. The use of some tools promotes direct expression, while others demand planning ahead and conceptual thinking. Sometimes these characteristics can be combined. One place this happens is in the printmaking workshop. In order to make a print, the artist must both conceptualize and apply tactile knowledge. His or her ideas and thoughts must be translated into something that can be realized using the technology at hand: some form of machine.

We perceive the world around us in different ways: sounds and smells, physical and visual sensations. In the brain we humans order our impressions and try to make sense of them. Artists do not only that; they aim to *create sense* as well. Our thoughts are not confined to words and grammar. We can use all sorts of different ways of thinking, just like we can use all sorts of tools in the studio or in the workshop. Machinery is prevalent – but not necessary. Regardless of what techniques they use, all artists aim to create work which will stir viewers' thoughts and emotions. Work which will be productive in the beholder's imagination, work for which there will never be a final answer but which will keep on raising new questions. We all aim to create works which will become Thought Machines.

Printmaking is the primordial Media Art, whose development began hundreds of years ago in the search for new means of distributing ideas, images and intuitions. Today, while many of its original functions have been taken up and industrialized in society at large, it remains one of the most potent platforms for artistic expression: rich in tradition while at the same time closely connected to the vanguard of technological innovation. This exhibition offers a panoply of experimental work by young artists based in Bratislava, Budapest, Leipzig, London and Vienna. Most of them study printmaking, some use it as a platform – and the work they show here is all concerned with the concept of Thought Machines.

This exhibition has come about thanks to a network of friendships and relationships between teachers and professors at the five participating institutions. Now we hope that this networking will be continued and expanded by their students. The first idea for a project was born during a visit to Budapest in spring of 2012, where two of my students participated in an exhibition organised by Professor Tibor Somorjai Kiss at the Hungarian University of Fine Arts. The plans became more concrete a little later when a whole group from Vienna spent a day at the Academy of Fine Arts and Design in Bratislava and were greeted there by Professor Róbert Jančovič. Expanding the exhibition's scope westward, I asked Professor Katrin von Maltzahn at the Academy of Visual Arts in Leipzig if she would like to participate. She, in turn, proposed we invite Professor Joanna Stockham and her students at the Royal College of Art in London. The title – Thought Machines – was coined by Katrin von Maltzahn. When Joanna Stockham heard about the special character of the spaces offered by the Heiligenkreuzerhof exhibition centre, she said: "Let's make an exhibition without walls!"

A concept was born. In January 2013 our students were invited, in a short text written by myself, to submit proposals on the theme of Thought Machines. Eighty-five proposals were presented. During a long day in Vienna in May 2013, the five of us made the selection decisions together.

The result of the process is documented in this catalogue and, more importantly, in the exhibition space itself. There are indeed works which are still presented on the walls, while others command the three-dimensional space between them, on the floor or hanging from the ceiling. All works relate to the concept of Thought Machines, which each time resonates differently depending on the particular angle from which each individual artist has chosen to approach it. The exhibition is an adventure, which you are now invited to become a part of!

I cannot mention everyone who has helped make this project a reality, but would like to extend my special thanks to my four international partners for their great co-operation and for their answers to my questions in the FAQ part of this catalogue; to my colleague in Vienna Attila Piller whose enthusiasm for a joint exhibition project with Budapest and Bratislava set the ball rolling; to Theresa Hattinger who designed the catalogue; to Christopher Barber who has been busy correcting our English – and to president Gerald Bast of the University of Applied Arts Vienna for supporting the project from the outset and funding the catalogue.

Finally and most importantly, I would like to thank the artists who have installed their Thought Machines. May they never stop

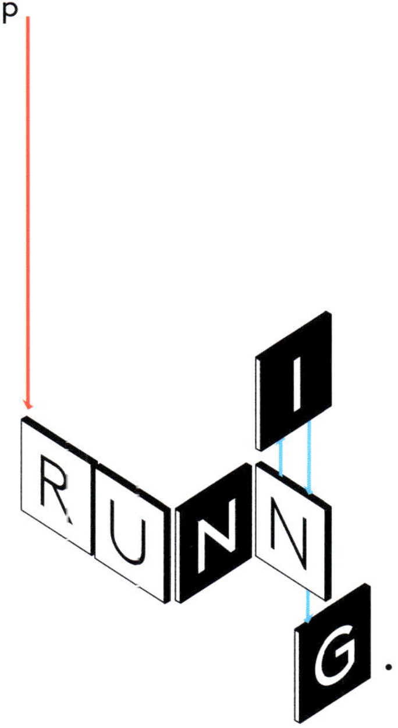

REFEKTORIUM

p.60
DE PHILIP POPPEK

p.32
GB WEIXIN CHONG
JAMES CHEEN FUEN SEOW

p.72
GB SHARON WHYTE

p.68
SK PAVOL TRUBEN

p.36
DE MAIKE DENKER

p.58
GB HANS-JÖRG POCHMANN

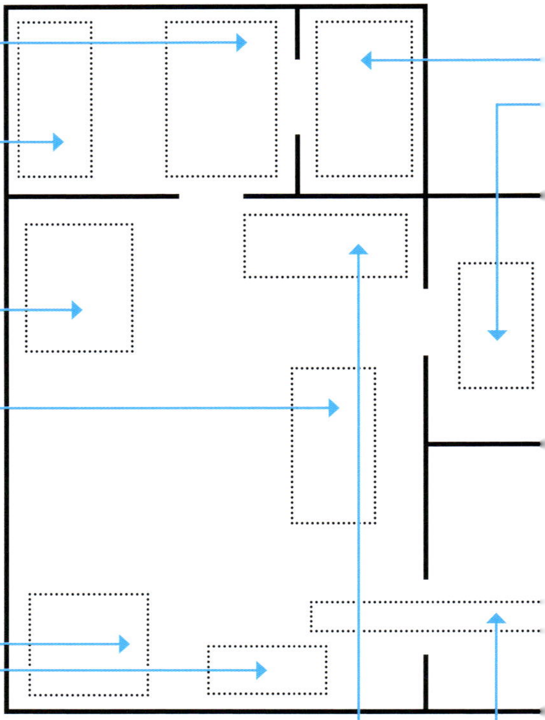

p.40
DE BENJAMIN DITTRICH

p.52
DE JULIAN IRLINGER

p.50
AT SIMON GORITSCHNIG

p.48
HU PÉTER GALLOV
PATRÍCIA JAGICZA

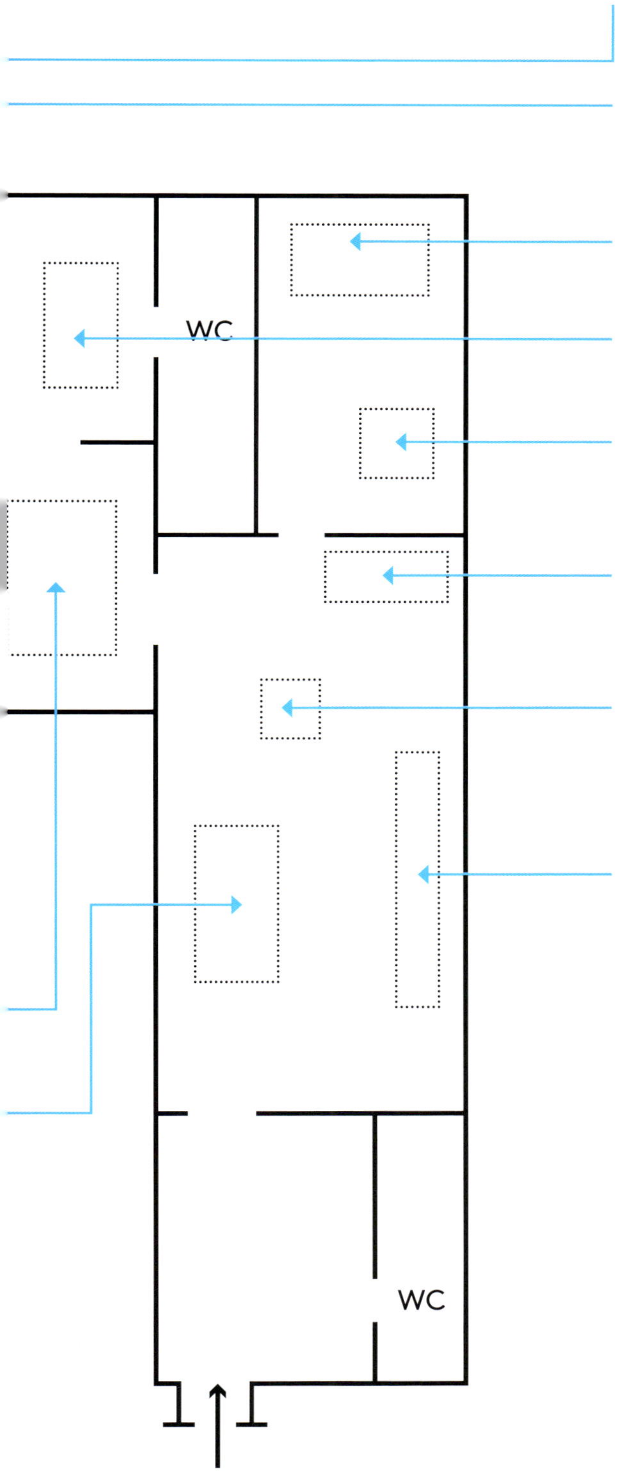

p. 62
GB MEG RAHAIM

p. 54
HU KATA MORAVSZKI
PÉTER ÜVEGES

p. 44
AT JASMIN EDELBRUNNER

p. 38
HU ADRIENN DÉR

p. 64
DE ROBERT SCHWARK

p. 70
HU RÉKA VIDRA

p. 46
SK SOŇA FLAJŽÍKOVÁ
JAKUB LOBOTKA

p. 26
AT JEREMIAS ALTMANN

SALA TERRENA

p.66
HU LÍDIA TAKÁCS

p.34
AT RENATA DARABANT

p.56
AT XENIA OSTROVSKAYA

p.42
AT BARTOSZ DOLHUN

p.74
DE SUSAN WINTER

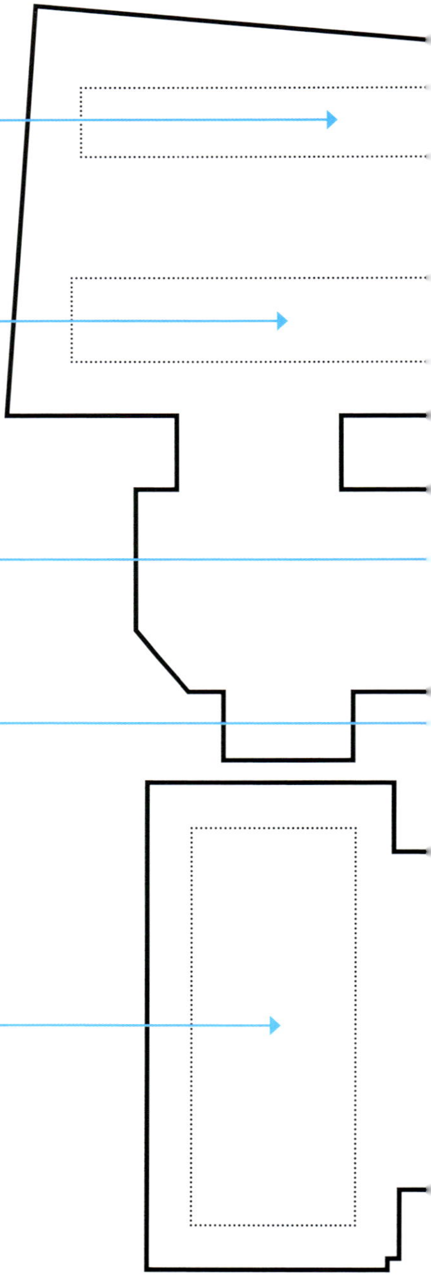

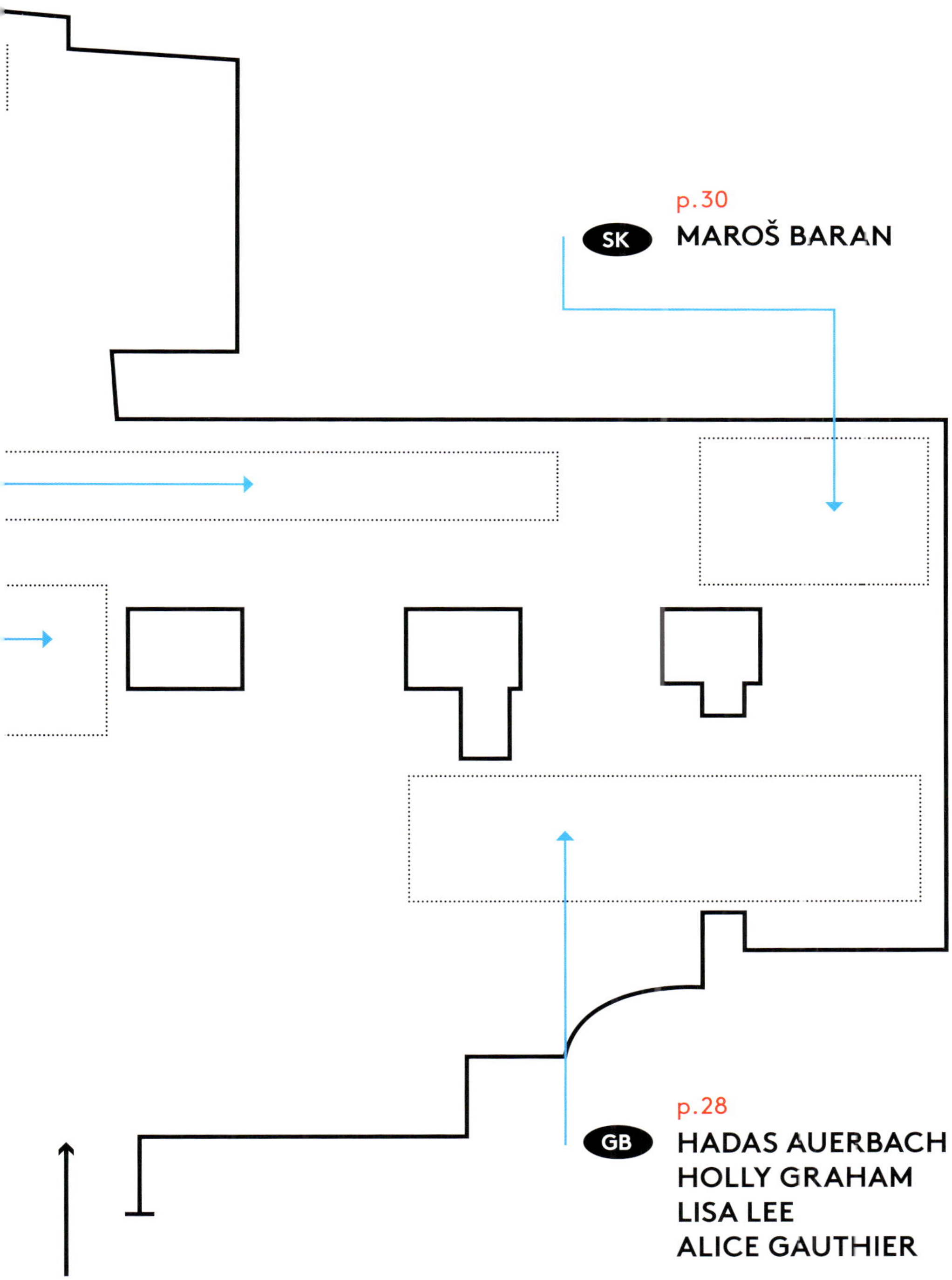
p.30
SK
MAROŠ BARAN
p.28
GB
HADAS AUERBACH
HOLLY GRAHAM
LISA LEE
ALICE GAUTHIER

ARTISTS

p.26

AT **JEREMIAS ALTMANN**
*1989 Vienna | Austria
University of Applied Arts Vienna
jerrino@gmx.at

p.28

GB **HADAS AUERBACH**
*1988 Tel Aviv | Israel
Royal College of Art, London
www.hadasauerbach.tumblr.com

ALICE GAUTHIER
*1989 Paris | France
Royal College of Art, London
www.gauthieralice.com

HOLLY GRAHAM
*1990 London | GB
Royal College of Art, London
www.hollygraham.co.uk

LISA LEE
*1986 Beijing | China
Royal College of Art, London
www.lisaleeart.com

p.30

SK **MAROŠ BARAN**
*1990 Bardejov | Slovakia
Academy of Fine Arts and Design, Bratislava
marosbaran.blogspot.sk

p.32

GB **WEIXIN CHONG**
*1989 Singapore
Royal College of Art, London
xiniary.wix.com/studio

JAMES CHEEN FUEN SEOW
*1971 Seremban, Malaysia
Royal College of Art, London
www.jamesseow.carbonmade.com

p.34

AT **RENATA DARABANT**
*1986 Oradea | Romania
University of Applied Arts Vienna
darabant.jimdo.com

p.36

DE

MAIKE DENKER

*1982 Münster | Germany
Academy of Visual Arts, Leipzig
www.cargocollective.com/maikedenker

p.38

HU

ADRIENN DÉR

*1988 Székesfehérvár | Hungary
Hungarian University of Fine Arts, Budapest
www.deradrienn.blogspot.com

p.40

DE

BENJAMIN DITTRICH

*1987 Düsseldorf | Germany
Academy of Visual Arts, Leipzig
www.benjamindittrich.de

p.42

AT

BARTOSZ DOLHUN

*1983 Lubin | Poland
University of Applied Arts Vienna
www.bartoszdolhun.com

p.43

AT

JASMIN EDELBRUNNER

*1983 Graz | Austria
University of Applied Arts Vienna
jasminedelbrunner.tumblr.com

p.46

SK

SOŇA FLAJŽÍKOVÁ

*1989 Skalica | Slovakia
Academy of Fine Arts and Design, Bratislava
www.behance.net/sonda

JAKUB LOBOTKA

*1986 Trenčín | Slovakia
Academy of Fine Arts and Design, Bratislava
www.behance.net/jalobotka

ARTISTS

p.48

HU
PÉTER GALLOV
*1984 Budapest | Hungary
Hungarian University of Fine Arts, Budapest

PATRÍCIA JAGICZA
*1986 Budapest | Hungary
Hungarian University of Fine Arts, Budapest
patriciajagicza.tumblr.com

p.50

AT
SIMON GORITSCHNIG
*1988 Klagenfurt | Austria
University of Applied Arts Vienna
www.simongoritschnig.com

p.52

DE
JULIAN IRLINGER
*1986 Erlangen | Germany
Academy of Visual Arts, Leipzig
j.irlinger@web.de

p.54

HU
KATA MORAVSZKI
*1992 Székesfehérvár | Hungary
Hungarian University of Fine Arts, Budapest
katamoravszki.tumblr.com

PÉTER ÜVEGES
*1991 Budapest | Hungary
Hungarian University of Fine Arts, Budapest
www.behance.net/uvegespeter

p.56

AT
XENIA OSTROVSKAYA
*1989 Leningrad | Russia
University of Applied Arts Vienna
www.xeniaostrovskaya.com

p.58

GB
HANS-JÖRG POCHMANN
*1984 Borna | Germany
Royal College of Art, London
www.hinojo.de

p.60

DE

PHILIP POPPEK

*1987 Berlin | Germany

Academy of Visual Arts, Leipzig

www.philippoppek.com

p.62

GB

MEG RAHAIM

*1980 Wilmington, Delaware | USA

Royal College of Art, London

www.megrahaim.com

p.64

DE

ROBERT SCHWARK

*1983 Burgstädt | Germany

Academy of Visual Arts, Leipzig

www.cossen.de

p.66

HU

LÍDIA TAKÁCS

*1989 Budapest | Hungary

Hungarian University of Fine Arts, Budapest

takacslidia.blogspot.com

p.68

SK

PAVOL TRUBEN

*1985 Žiar nad Hronom | Slovakia

Academy of Fine Arts and Design, Bratislava

www.pavoltruben.eu

p.70

HU

RÉKA VIDRA

*1990 Szolnok | Hungary

Hungarian University of Fine Arts, Budapest

www.behance.net/vidrareka

p.72

GB

SHARON WHYTE

*1972 Edinburgh | Scotland

Royal College of Art, London

www.sharonwhyte.co.uk

p.74

DE

SUSAN WINTER

*1972 Riesa | Germany

Academy of Visual Arts, Leipzig

FAQ

1 WHAT IS YOUR MOTIVATION FOR PRINTMAKING?*

GB JOANNA STOCKHAM
Professor, Head of Printmaking
Royal College of Art, London

I have always been obsessed with images of all kinds. The possibility of making them with processes which allow for repetition, change and chance intervention, for the transformation of the same image onto different materials and at different scales, creates a wealth of possibilities which excite me. The way in which the nuances of different surfaces complicate and slow down our response to something made or found fascinates me. There is a democracy in using and circulating images which can be distributed freely and placed in multiple spaces outside the gallery, in publications, or on the street.

HU TIBOR SOMORJAI KISS
Professor, Rector,
Head of the Graphics Department/
Specialization in Graphic Arts
Hungarian University of Fine Arts,
Budapest

It is not only the possibility of multiplication that appeals to me, but also the quality of dots and lines that can be created with the given technique. As a result of the technical parameters of printmaking as such, the possibilities of variation with regard to the prints produced create new visual ideas.

* Jan Svenungsson's questions were sent via email in June. These are the full answers; they were not coordinated in advance.

AT JAN SVENUNGSSON

Professor, Head of the Department
for Graphics and Printmaking
University of Applied Arts Vienna

To me, making art is exploration. I want to learn new things and I want to be surprised by the consequences of my ideas and intuitions. Printmaking in its many forms provides particular tools with which this can take place. When you are making a print, the process must be planned in advance and in several stages. But you never know whether the map you have made can be trusted, and thus you must remain ever vigilant throughout the trip. You must be ready to adjust course, change tack, gather discoveries. If all goes well, the journey will end with a new departure.

DE KATRIN VON MALTZAHN

Professor for Printmaking,
Department of Painting / Graphic Arts
Academy of Visual Arts, Leipzig

Developing an idea into a print suits my working approach. I enjoy experiencing the gap between planning and intuition. The process can unify the whole history of image production: one can start with a photograph, continue with digital image processing, then manually work on the plate, perhaps add lettering, and finish by printing on a 150-year-old press and receive a contemporary image.

Teaching in the field of printmaking offers great opportunities for dealing with artistic questions in relation to contemporary visual media and culture.

SK RÓBERT JANČOVIČ

Professor, Head of the Department
for Printmaking and Other Media
Academy of Fine Arts and Design,
Bratislava

It is the transformation process of an intangible idea/thought/message, which evolves on a tangible platform – a matrix – and consequently returns again as an immaterial message, a concept.

FAQ

2 WHAT ROLE DOES PRINTMAKING PLAY WITHIN CONTEMPORARY ART & HOW DO YOU SEE ITS FUTURE?

DE **KVM:** Today a variety of artists not traditionally seen as printmakers make prints. Among them are filmmakers, conceptual artists, sculptors and installation artists who use traditional printmaking techniques as an autonomous part of their artistic production. A new wave of artists coming from painting and drawing are beginning to create original works in print – often in large dimensions. Frequently their primary motivation is not the possibility of producing editions. Instead they may feel drawn to particular tactile qualities in the final image, or it is the character of the working process that draws them in.

On the one hand, the wealth of digital images is causing a revival of traditional hands-on-techniques among artists. On the other hand, digital technologies expand printmaking: photography and 3-D processes become printmaking.

HU **TSK:** The appreciation of individual graphic works made with traditional printmaking techniques has perceptibly declined and been relegated to the domain of Hungarian and international biennials. Presently, technical boundaries are blurred in mainstream art; graphic art is sometimes used as a supplementary component of mixed media.

GB **JS:** Printmaking is central to the practises of many contemporary artists who would not describe themselves as printmakers. Artists' use of archives, the rise of work using algorithms and data transformation, and the growth in self-publishing have, alongside a growing interest in simple hand-crafts such as woodcut and screen-print, all contributed to the widespread use of print. I believe this trend will continue to grow as the dominance of technology, including its normative and controlling aspects, causes people to seek other tools of production or other ways of using those tools. The constant demand that people represent themselves via social media also creates an urgent need to understand the way images can be read, and the way they circulate meaning and affect.

SK **RJ:** The role depends on each individual; it's the role each one assigns to this medium. It is idea, message, enthusiasm that usually "win". The way the image is produced doesn't determine how contemporary and up-to-date the final artwork is. The longevity of printmaking, of its principles and procedures, is ensured by its ability to reflect us human beings and the world around us, and by its ability to absorb new trends and technologies. I'm not worried about printmaking's future. I'm more concerned about other factors influencing our world. There are more important questions.

AT **JS:** The technology of digital printmaking is becoming ever more dominant in contemporary art production. Today, many artists – photographers, painters, whoever – prepare their images on the computer. And very often they print them using digital technology, either as the finished product or as a step in the creative process. In effect they have joined the ranks of printmakers. It's a growth area, at least in quantitative terms.

3 WHAT DIFFERENCE DOES IT MAKE, USING DIGITAL OR ANALOG TOOLS FOR PRINTMAKING?

SK **RJ:** I think the main tool remains the human being, the human brain, our ability to reflect ourselves and the world around us. All the rest are just associated phenomena.

Although the visual appearance of a work of art is determined by the way it was created, this will influence the main idea only to a certain extent. Nevertheless, there are artists who will consider the process itself to be the most important part of the artwork.

AT **JS:** The main difference involves how mistakes occur, what role they play and what kind of meaning they produce. There are tactile aspects of making and correcting mistakes in an analogue process that may never be translatable into language. On the computer all action is based upon commands, in other words upon language.

Personally I feel very attracted to analogue printmaking processes because of the balancing act between planning, making and mistaking – which cannot, in the end, be rendered in language.

HU **TSK:** Digital procedures are a plus, enriching the repertoire of printmaking tools. The role of the manual approach has decreased considerably, and simultaneously prints have more become compilations of ready-made visual elements.

GB **JS:** In our workshops any image which includes a photographic or textual element now almost always has a digital component, even if just as an intermediary film state. For me the manual handling of material, cutting, collaging and drawing allow for a slower reflective space than is possible on the computer, which I find to be an instrument of constant distraction. Personally I build images a little like I build installations, like montages in a way. Digital scanning and the processes of enlarging and cropping in Photoshop allow new approaches to working with the enlarged fragment, and this reveals things differently from analogue magnification both in terms of the subject and the limitations of the tools.

DE **KVM:** In analogue printmaking you don't see the image before all technical steps have been carried out. Analogue tools are more dirty and the manual work takes more time (especially when the print is multicoloured). The human factor can lead to accidents which may influence artistic decision-making and its outcome. In digital printmaking the image exists on the computer screen before it is printed. It is possible to simulate analogue printmaking by the choice of material.

FAQ

4 WHAT IS YOUR NOTION OF A THOUGHT MACHINE – IN RELATION TO YOUR OWN WORK, TO YOUR TEACHING OR WORKSHOP EXPERIENCES?

HU **TSK:** The Thought Machine project provides an opportunity for visual thinking that points beyond the boundaries of traditional graphics and facilitates the analysis of the printmaking process.

AT **JS:** I am convinced that the best works of art are those which continue over time to trigger ever new thoughts and questions in their viewers, and in their makers as well. Such works don't offer themselves for easy consumption, and they do not dull with time. We artists continuously face the challenge of building such Thought Machines and figuring out their mechanisms – although we never will completely.

DE **KVM:** A "Thought Machine" as a trigger for ideas: Printmaking demands planning ahead. Its processes take time and demand a focus on technical rules – this opens space for artistic thinking and unexpected solutions.

A "Thought Machine" as a trigger for contemporary cultural questions: Printmaking was always connected to the latest technologies and to important cultural developments. Today the old inventions encounter contemporary questions relating to basic cultural changes: the meaning of the original and the copy, the role of the author, the value of copyrights, the speed of the information flow, the value of physical material and production ...

GB **JS:** In my work I try to engage in my own act of playing with the process of looking and re-looking at images I have made or found and giving them a form or body available in some way to the viewer. In this way, thinking through making and feeling through making and reflecting upon the choices one makes is part of my work. In teaching I encourage students to embrace contradiction and the instability of images, particularly when they are multiplied and distributed outside the gallery.

At the RCA we embrace the often conflicting histories of printmaking; one with an emphasis on tradition and craft, and the other as an engagement with print media including the moving image and an emphasis on communication and graphics. Both areas collide in the making of books and in the use of text and image, where the histories of print itself are the ground for thinking of print as a thought machine.

The field interests me because the conceptual and the haptic can co-exist in all print media; a mind-body bridge. A reflective and experimental approach to work allows students to improvise within different situations and spaces, and this is the gift of the Thought Machines exhibition.

SK **RJ:** Each theme generates or modifies new inputs. The term "Thought Machine"? As far as I know, the most important "machine" is our brain, which remains a secret that is largely unexplored. It gives us freedom, but at the same time it creates boundaries. If we think of the brain as a never-ending universe, there is still a lot of work for us to do before we can fully dominate it.

TM550

AT JEREMIAS ALTMANN

Drawing, pencil on paper
(in cooperation with
Martin Bischof) and video

26

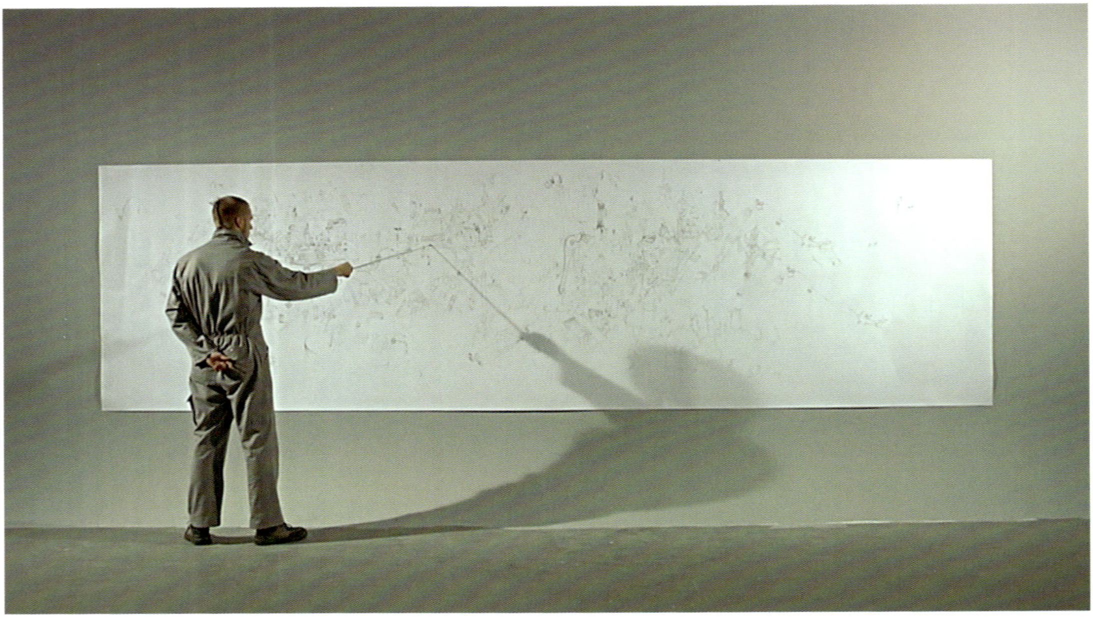

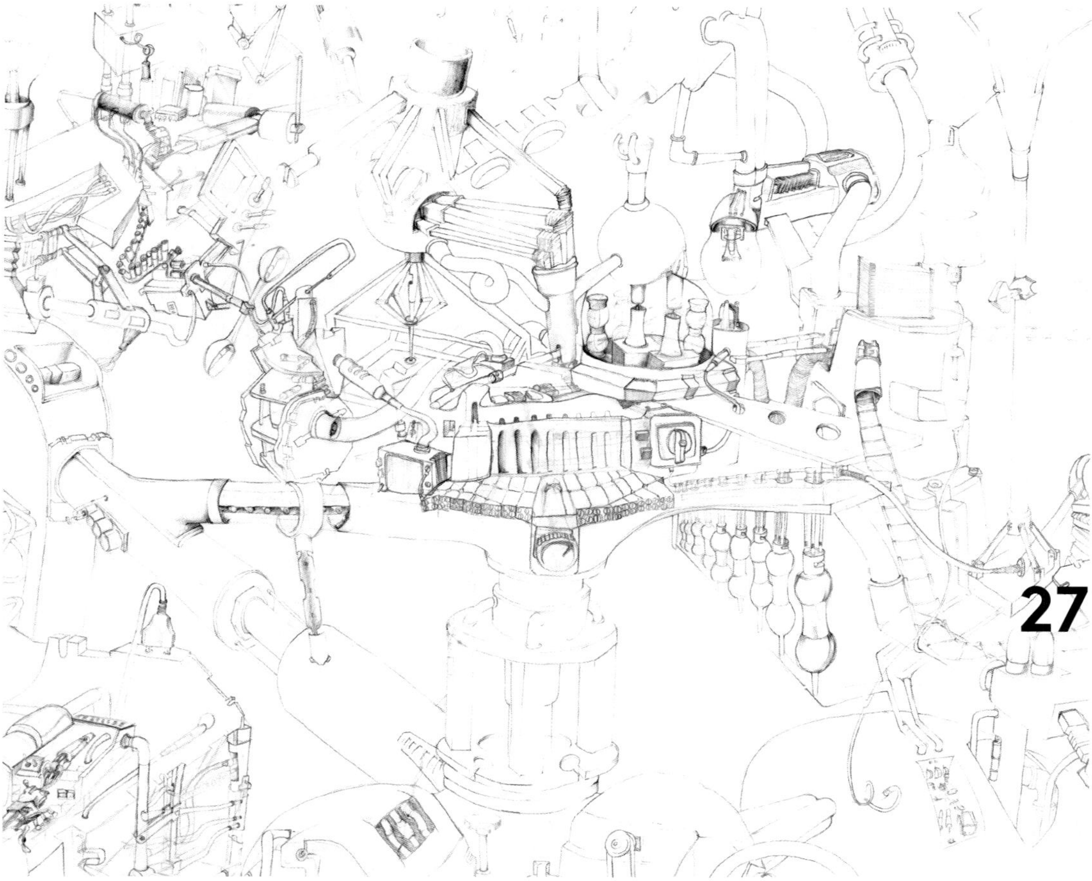

27

Why does no machine exist that can produce juice for all the children of the world from a single grape? TM550 – the end of this question.

DOWN TO EARTH

GB HADAS AUERBACH
ALICE GAUTHIER
HOLLY GRAHAM
LISA LEE

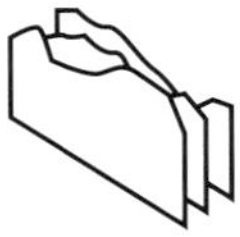

Torn screen prints
installed on floor

28

CLOUD:
noun

- a visible mass of condensed watery vapour floating in the atmosphere, typically high above the general level of the ground
- an indistinct or billowing mass

The blank page as a vehicle for thought
or as the cause of writer's block.
Our paper has absorbed the sky.
Let your mind wander through our
cloudscape.

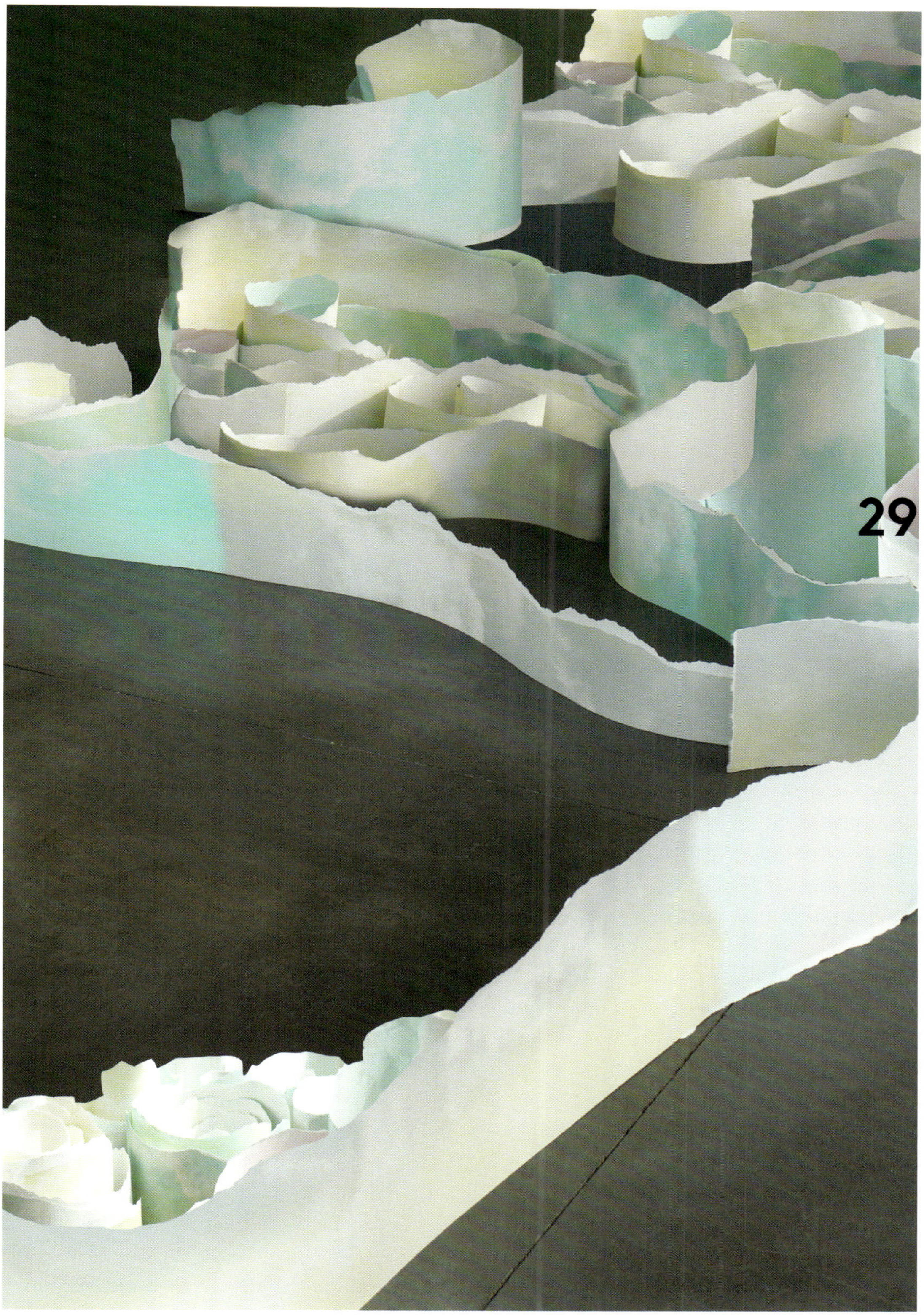

THE SILVER LAKE

SK MAROŠ BARAN

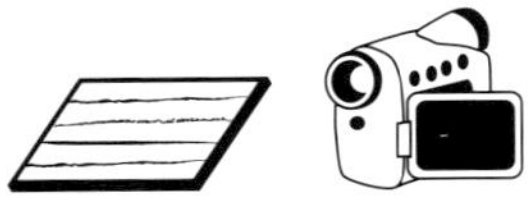

Floor installation
and video projection

30

In February 2013 I lost the most important person in my life. The violence of life struck me to the core. In my mourning days I realized that the greatest thinking machine, above all art and life, is Death itself. I cursed Death for many days, many weeks… but then I realized that although my friend is physically not with me any more, he is in my heart. I used to read this in books, but never really believed it could be true. Now I do.

Death is always there, but love and hope are as well. Below the surface lie animal skulls, overgrown by flowers that never wilt. Shining from below, showing beauty only after you begin “to care”. Without the power you invest, it is just fake water.

One shall find peace and silence, while looking for answers within questions.

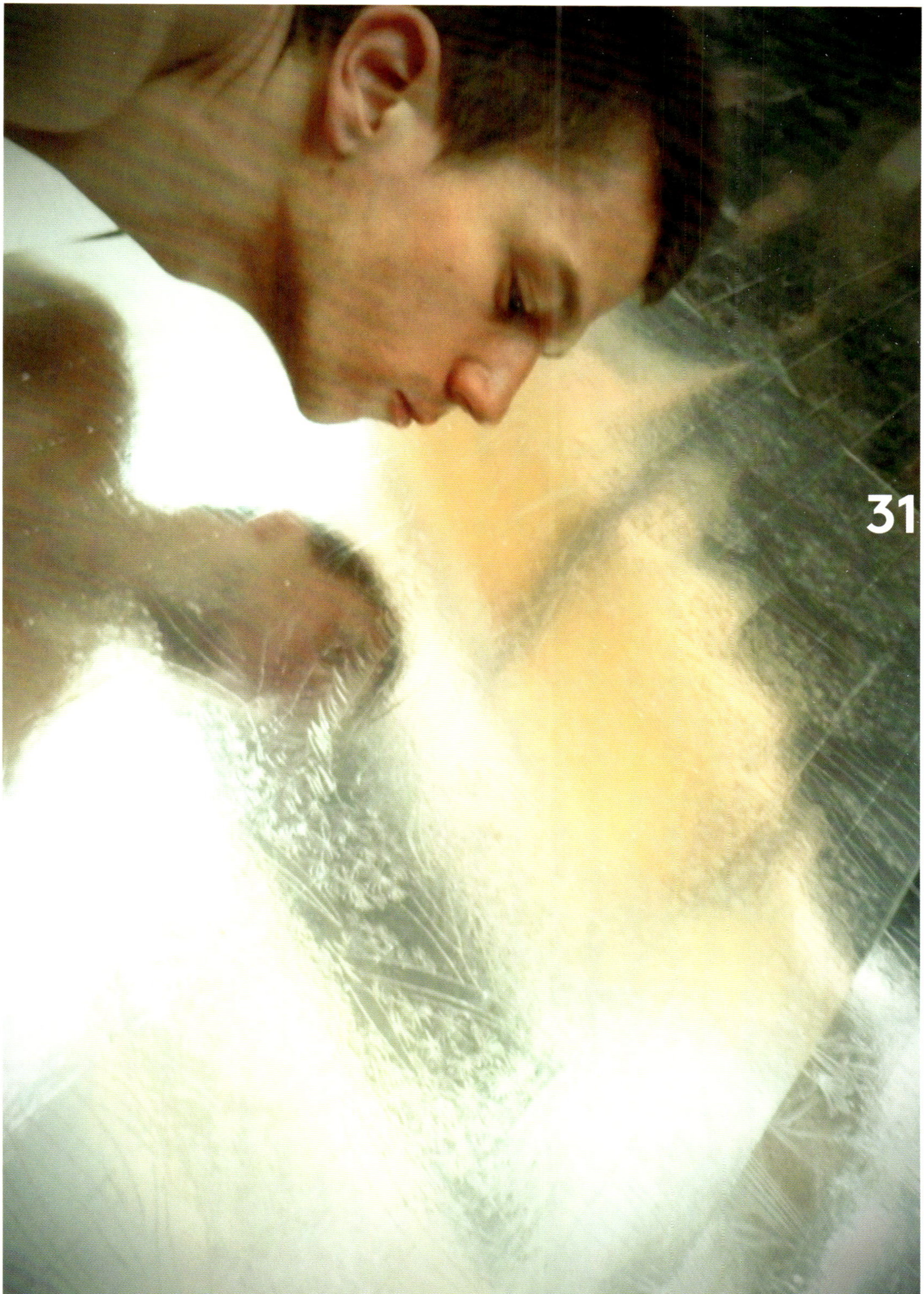

...NOW I WILL DO NOTHING BUT LISTEN

GB WEIXIN CHONG
JAMES CHEEN FUEN SEOW

Sound installation

32

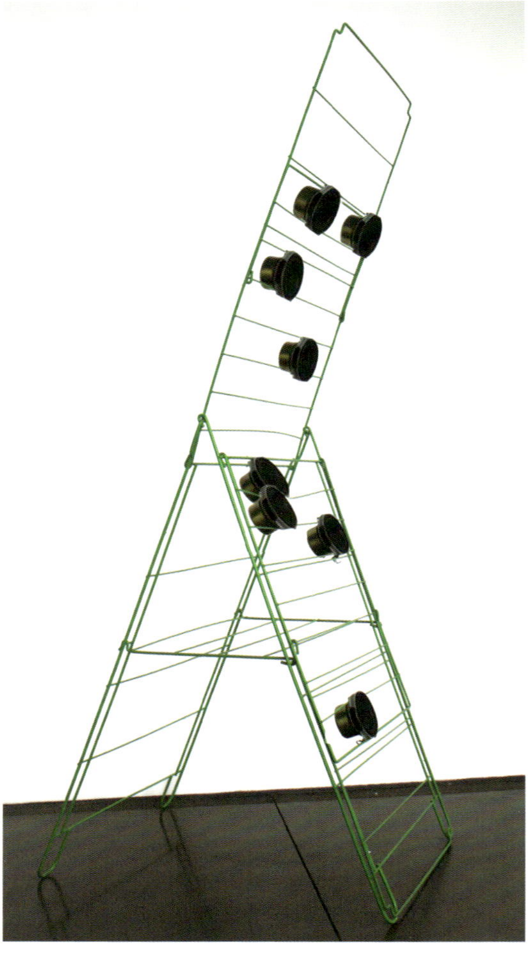

In the acoustic environment of a print-making workshop, a palette of sounds shape the unknown hours of labour and thought processes of making art.

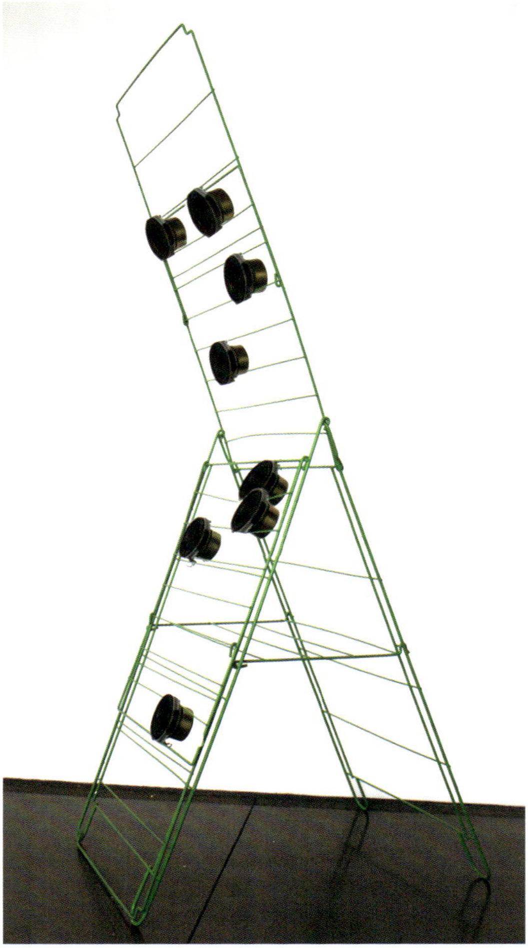

This installation is based on the recorded sound of limestone grinding using a levigator and carborundum grit, done at the Royal College of Art's lithography department.

Given the temporal nature of the contemporary attention span, one's impressions of artworks are continuously and rapidly replaced. The act of removing images from the stone resonates with the mental process of consuming.

REFLECTION

AT RENATA DARABANT

Drawings
(based on axial CT scans
licensed from the Visible
Human Project®, The U.S.
National Library of Medicine)

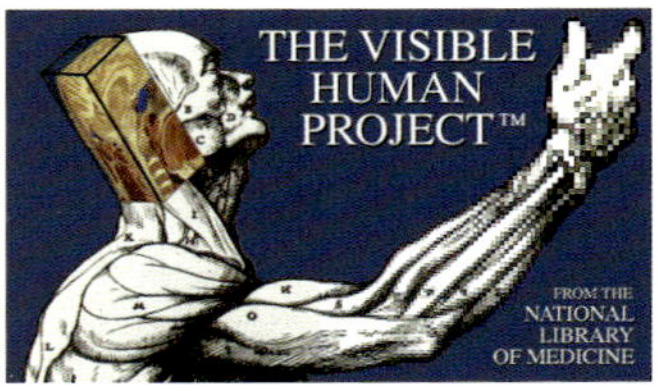

34

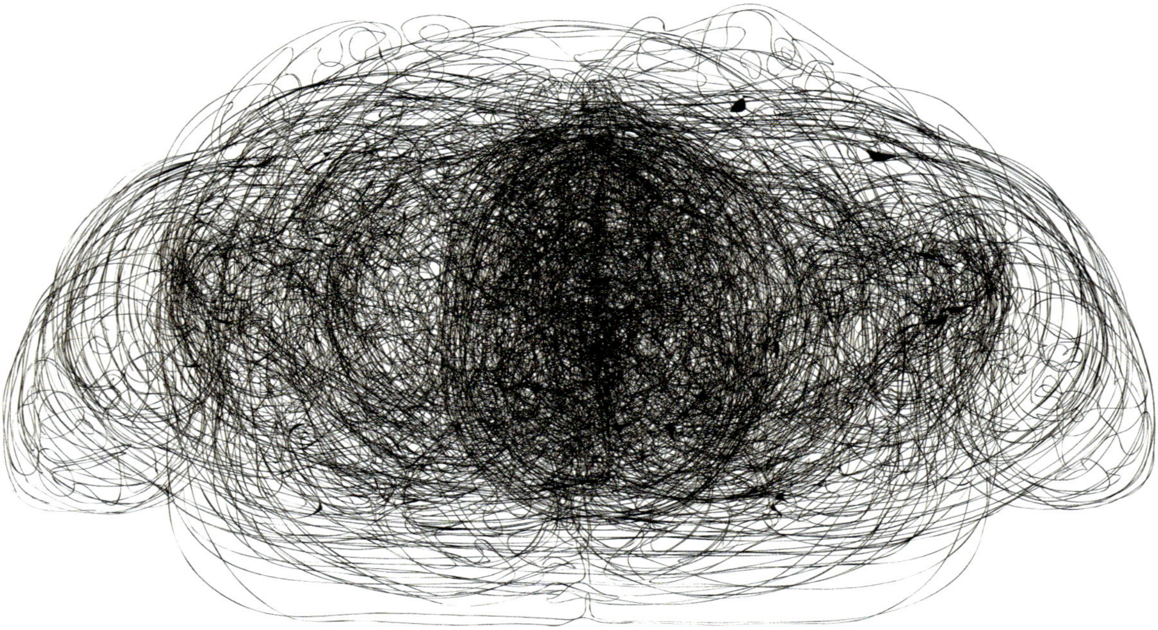

Are you curious about your inner life?
What defines you and how do you define yourself?
Are you more than the sum of your cells and thoughts?
Can you examine or determine your self?
Are you different from anybody?
What is your essence?
Who are you?

35

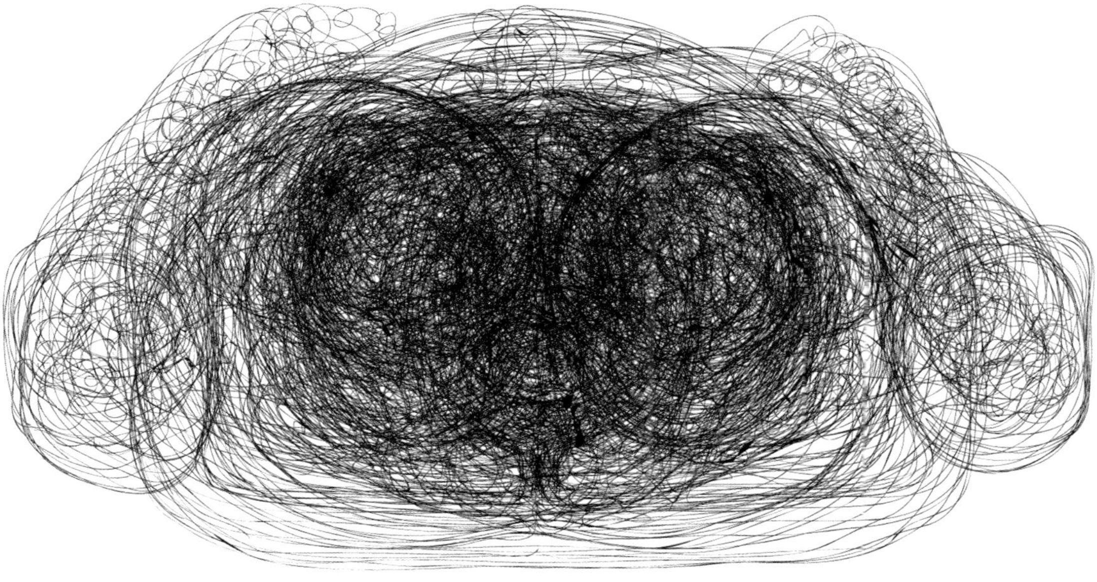

DE MAIKE DENKER

ANNIE & ELISABETH

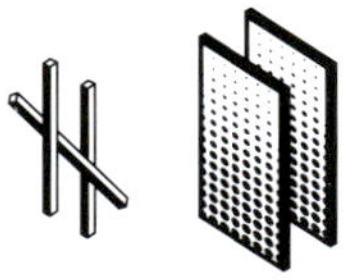

Metal construction and linocuts
(printed with an inherited wringer)

36

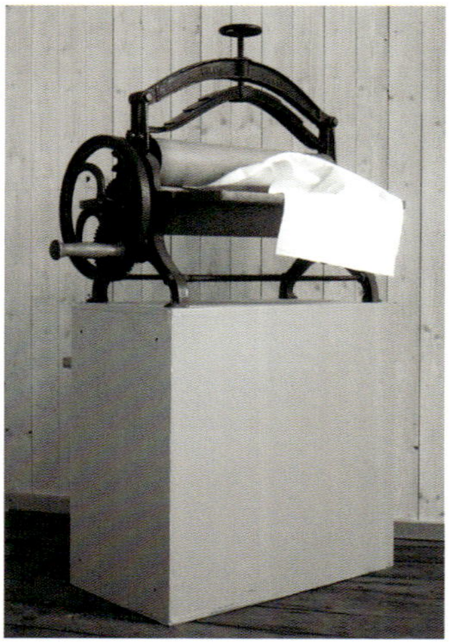

1. First, look out for the qualities of the object (and if you like, add some special features).
2. Then initiate the process by separating the artefacts.
3. Start the reproductive isolation (for remarkable results, let a slight disparity evolve in the form).
4. Do not forget to interpret the morphology and behaviour of the unusual.
5. After that you should expand your results (sometimes this process will be attended by inexplicable confusion).
6. But keep in mind: there is nothing for you to worry about, just go on with your research.

THE GAME IS OVER

HU ADRIENN DÉR

Installation

38

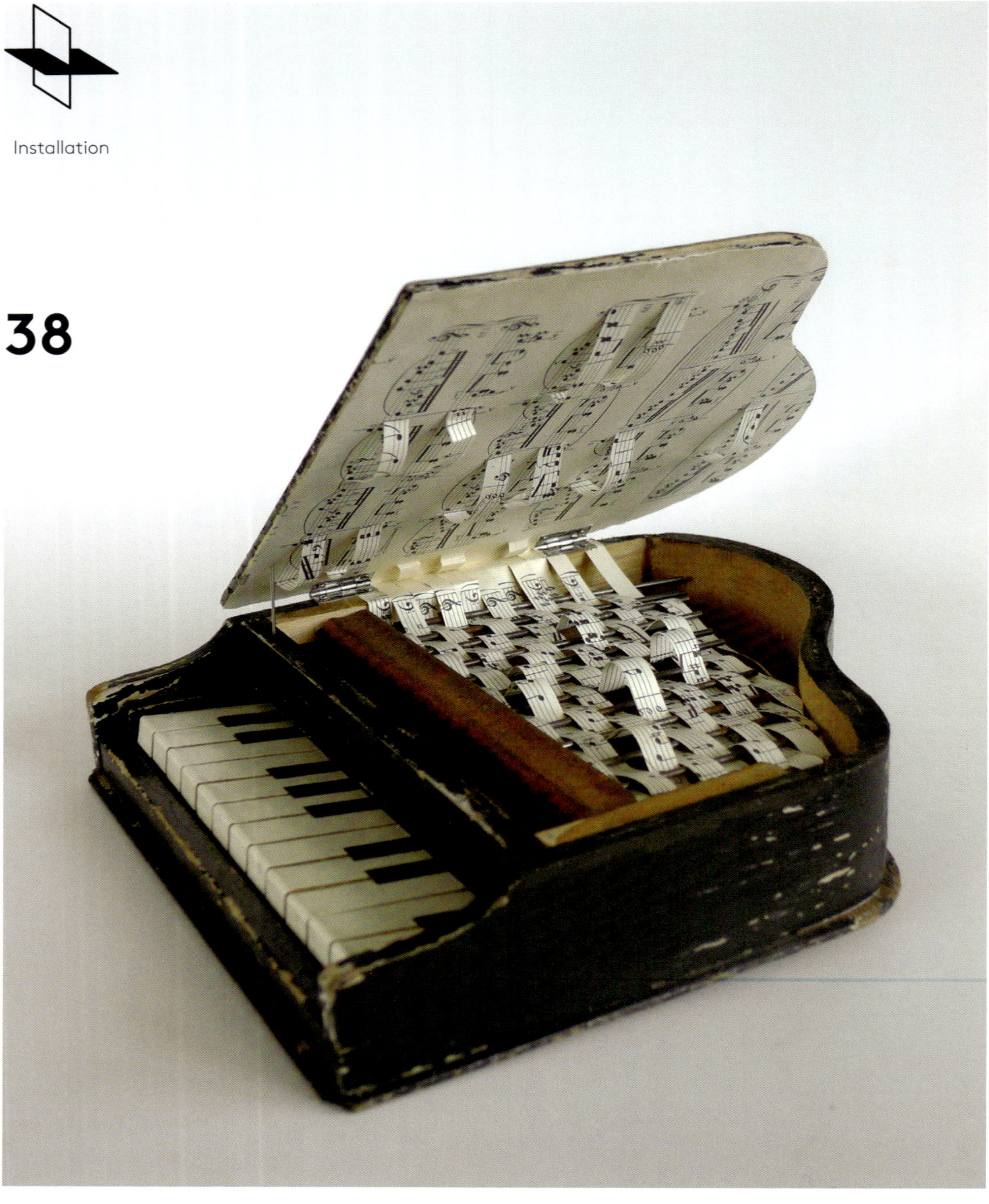

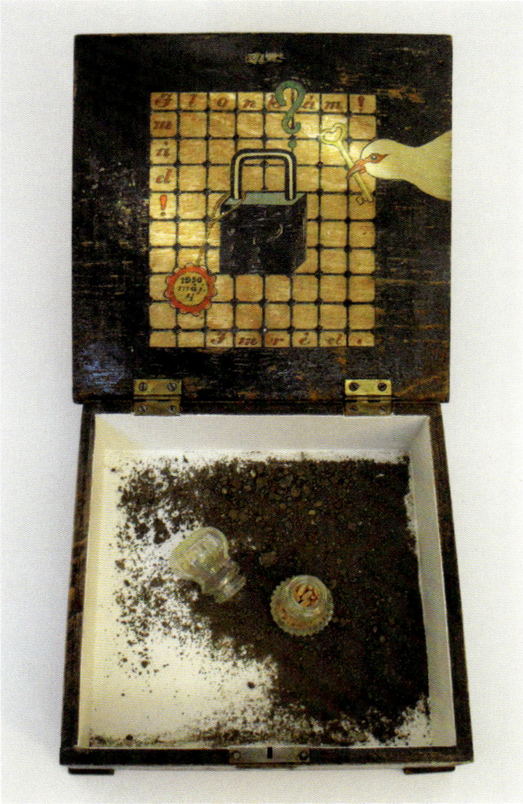

In October 2012 the Hungarian government banned the operation of gambling machines, except for those in casinos.

As a result of this ban, more than ten thousand people (including family members) lost their livelihood, and the state deprived itself of considerable tax revenue. This measure was justified from a sociological point of view. People living under precarious circumstances should not be allowed to spend their money on slot machines, and addiction to them poses a threat to national health.

Unfortunately, in spite of this prohibition, many citizens will still feel a need for these machines, and there will be significant illegal operation and trafficking. Thus the government will lose tax revenue.

We can see a complex set of problems here. I would like to comment on the situation through my work.

ORBIS PICTUS

DE **BENJAMIN DITTRICH**

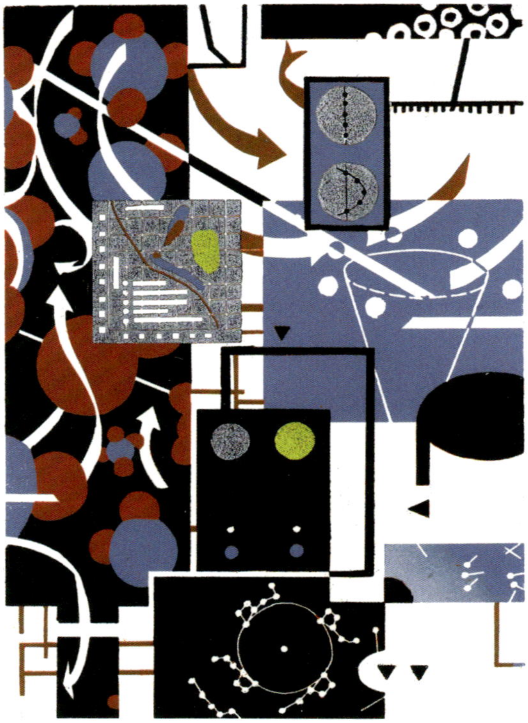

Linocuts

40

Reading it again, she realized how strange it sounded. Those beings' quest for knowledge was based on the search for similarities. Unimaginably, a world was created, which was not oriented around needs, but around the denotation of things. Extensively, it had been categorized, classified, catalogued. The pursuit of expectable certainties described seemed almost desperate to her. Out of a regime of sense, these diverse societies created an order of things, which could have only resulted in identity and difference. Yet most absurdly, the beings concerned reflected on these processes and knew about the home-made reign of unambiguity. The existing categories were understood, but instead of changing them they kept reproducing them. From this point forward, she read in disbelief, purely symbolic aesthetics were dominant. Knowledge became a contextless entity, consisting of fragmentary ornaments.

Max Haase

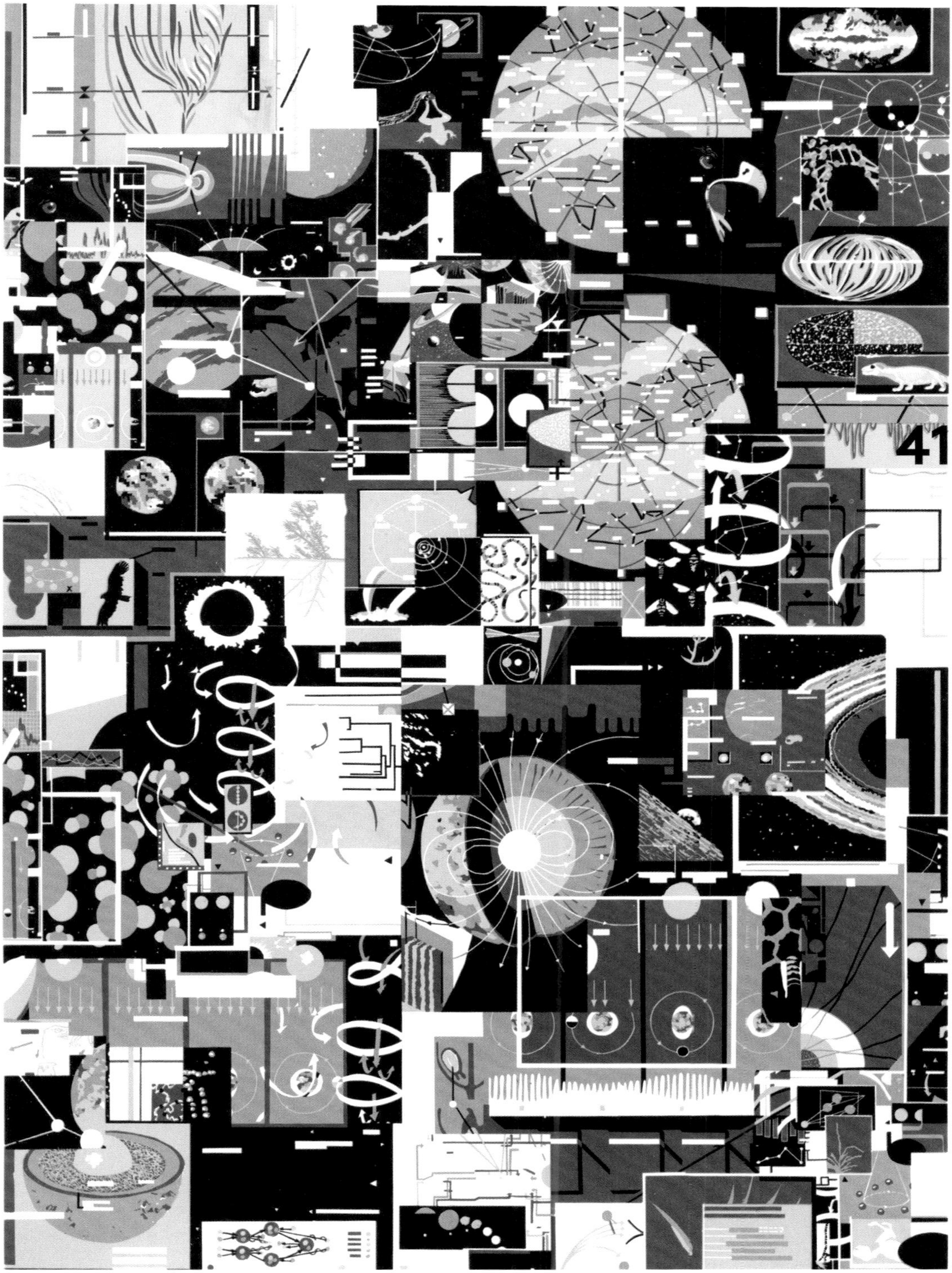
41

A DIME A THOUSAND

AT BARTOSZ DOLHUN

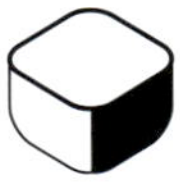

1000 printed
paving stones

42

Build your own individual and unique mini-BIGM★C paper model according to your needs.

1. Cut out the shape.
2. Fold the tabs by hand along the broken lines. You don't need to score them with any tool before.
3. Assemble the cube by gluing the tabs marked with an X.
4. Let the assembled cube dry.
5. Now scrunch up your BIGM★C-model. Don't rip it up.
6. Bring your scrunched model back to shape again.
7. Here you are! Your unique BIGM★C-model with a paving-stone look.
8. There is no reason why you can't make your BIGM★C bigger. Just enlarge it on your copying machine. Any copy of this model is desirable.

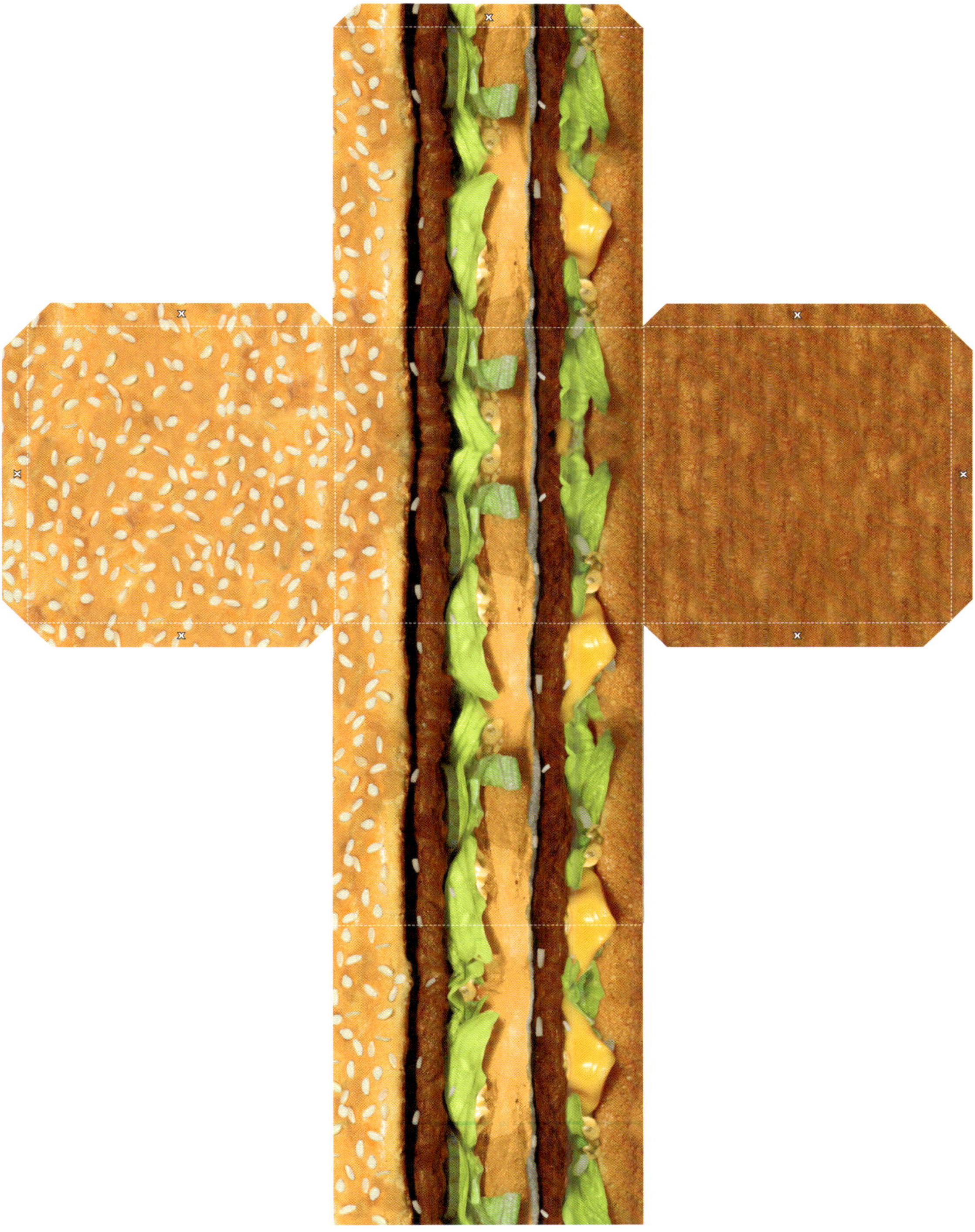

CIRCLES

AT JASMIN EDELBRUNNER

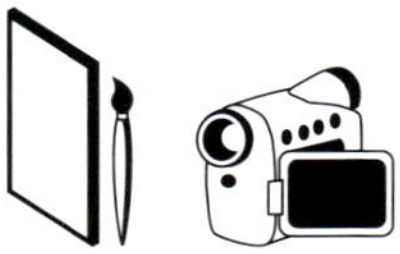

Installation with painting and video projection

44

The act of painting circles is reminiscent of machines repeating their sequences in an endless process. While painting one circle, I have already started the next one in my thoughts. Machines work like that – they create and finish at the same time.

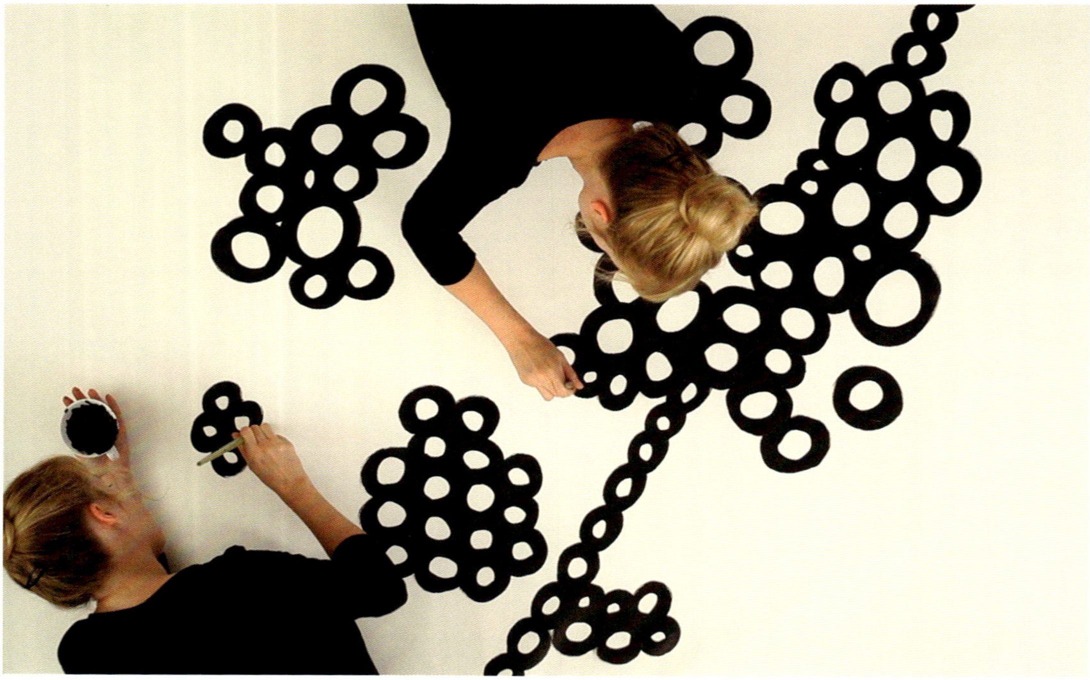

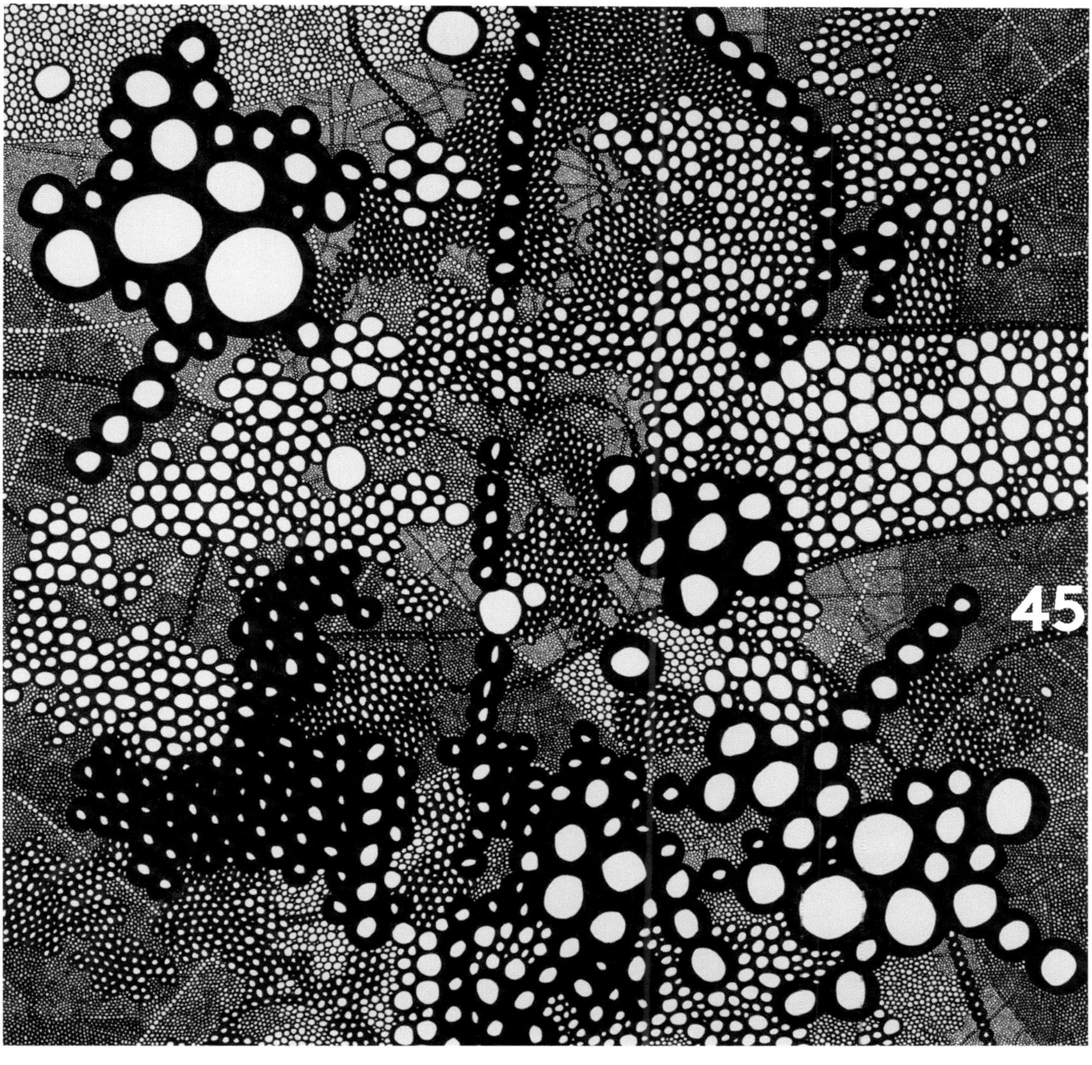

COLUMN OF VISUAL MEMORY

SK SOŇA FLAJŽÍKOVÁ
JAKUB LOBOTKA

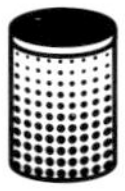

Steel cylinder with
applied print media

46

The installation refers to the columns for displaying posters that can be seen throughout the city. These eye-catchers are cylindrical and two meters high. The posters hung on them try to draw our attention every day.

We are basically imitating this object. We cover the cylinder with our own prints in layers as well as with mainstream print media, letting them communicate on one surface.

We would like to retain the original principle of layering posters, and also the information overkill and visual abuse of the public sometimes associated with such columns. When you hang a new poster in this type of public space, you are also covering an old one. This process of self-consuming images is represented in our work.

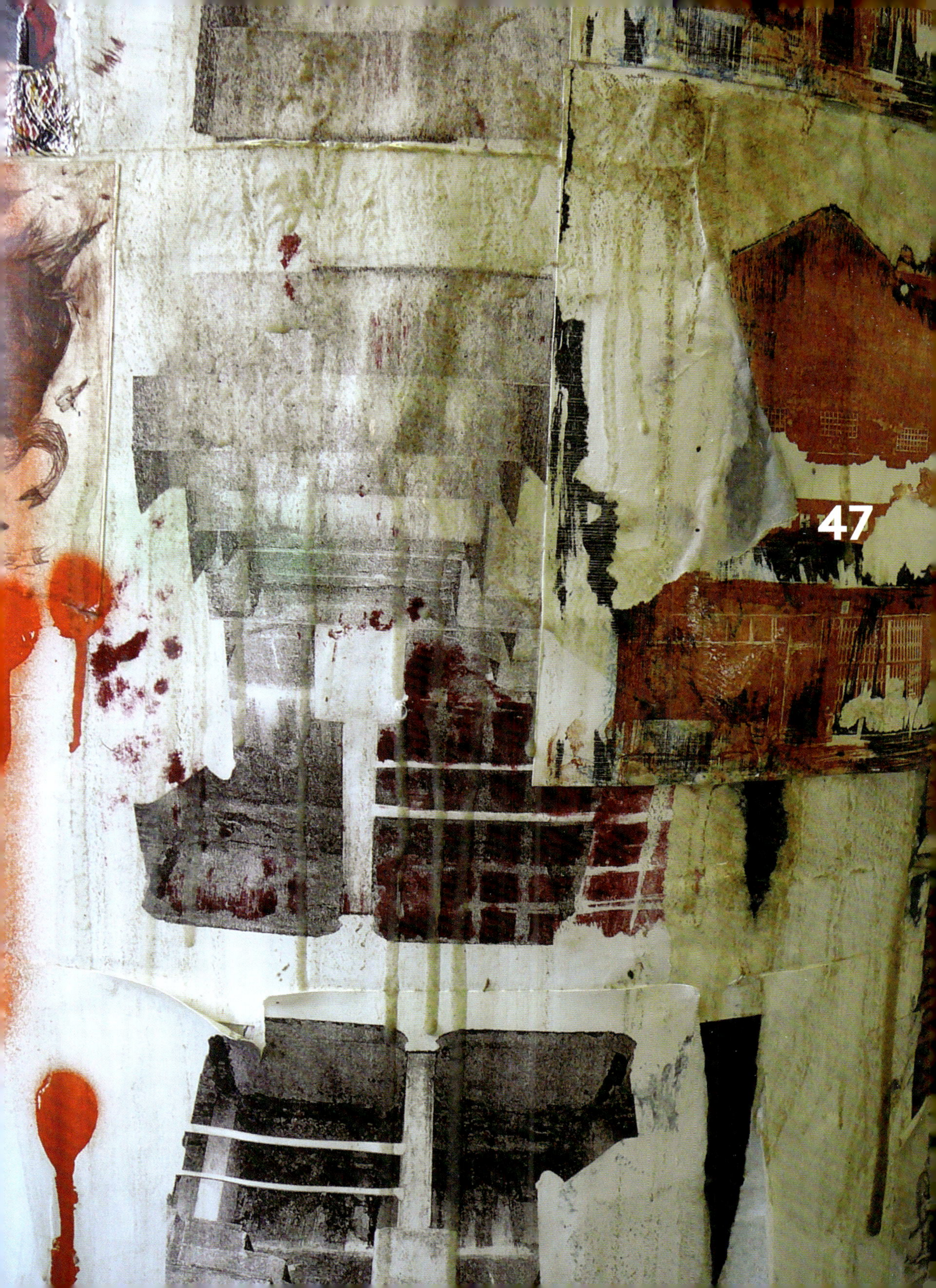

CHAT

HU PÉTER GALLOV
PATRÍCIA JAGICZA

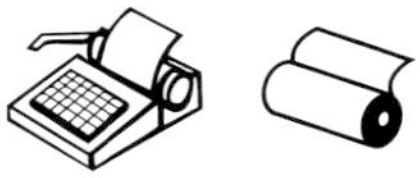

Installation with type-
writers and paper reels

48

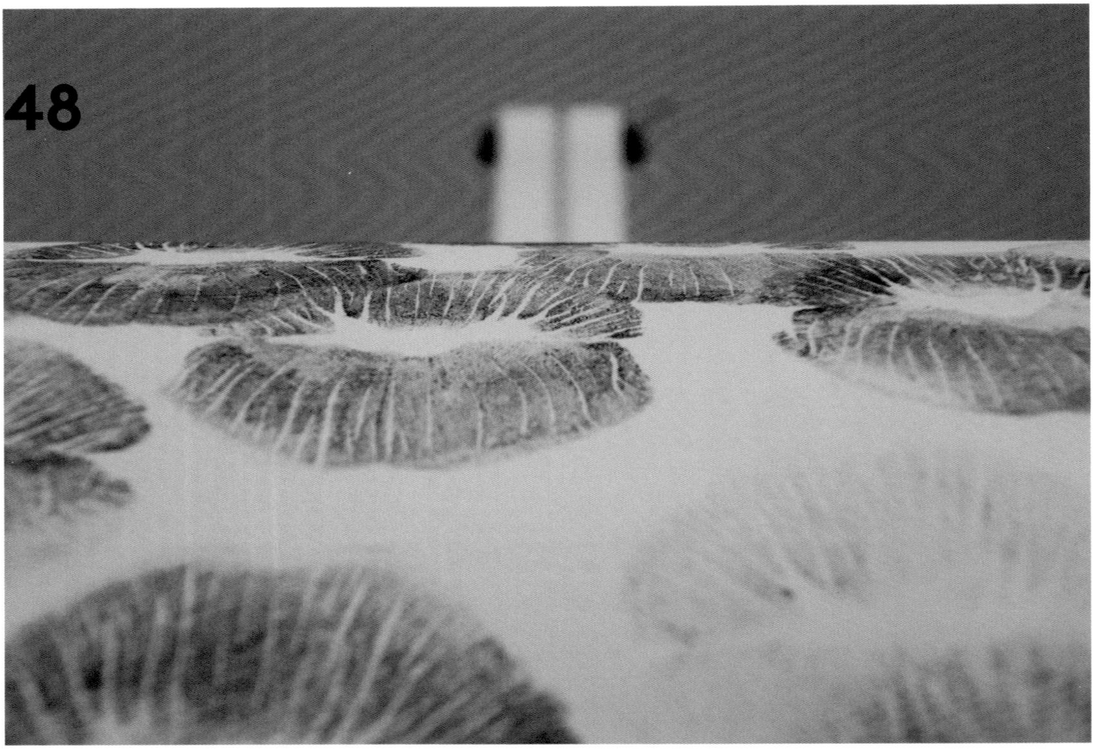

The machines communicate with each other through signals which they type onto a paper connecting them. The typewriters cannot be used in the normal fashion, because here they are merely components of the installation; this piece of art is not interactive.

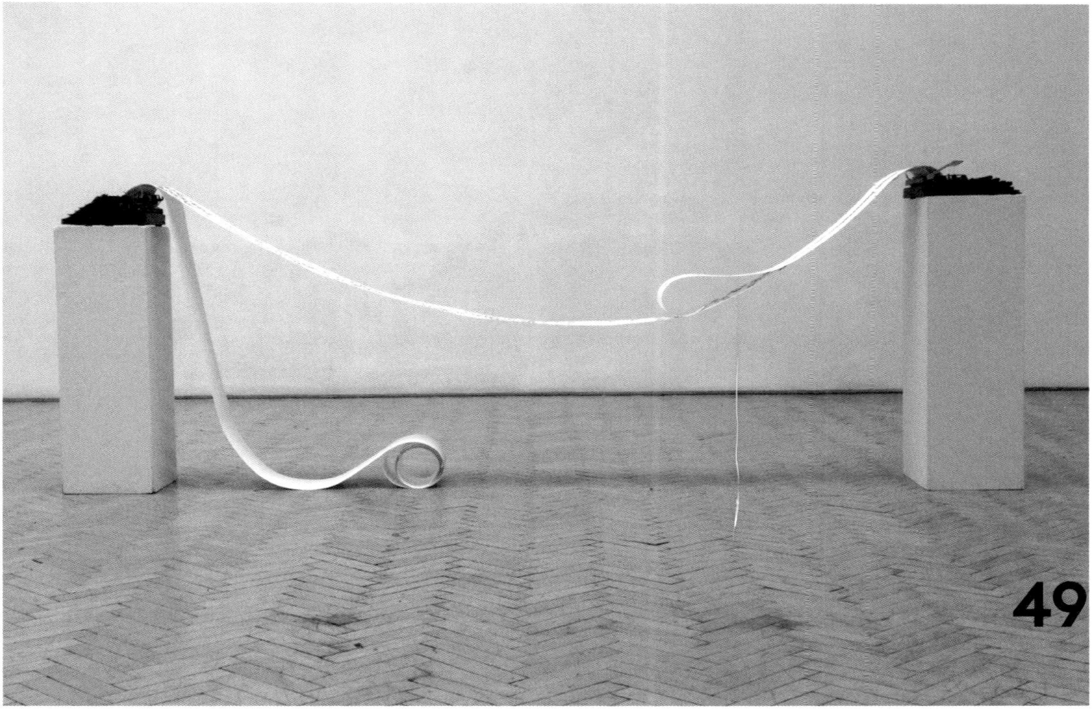

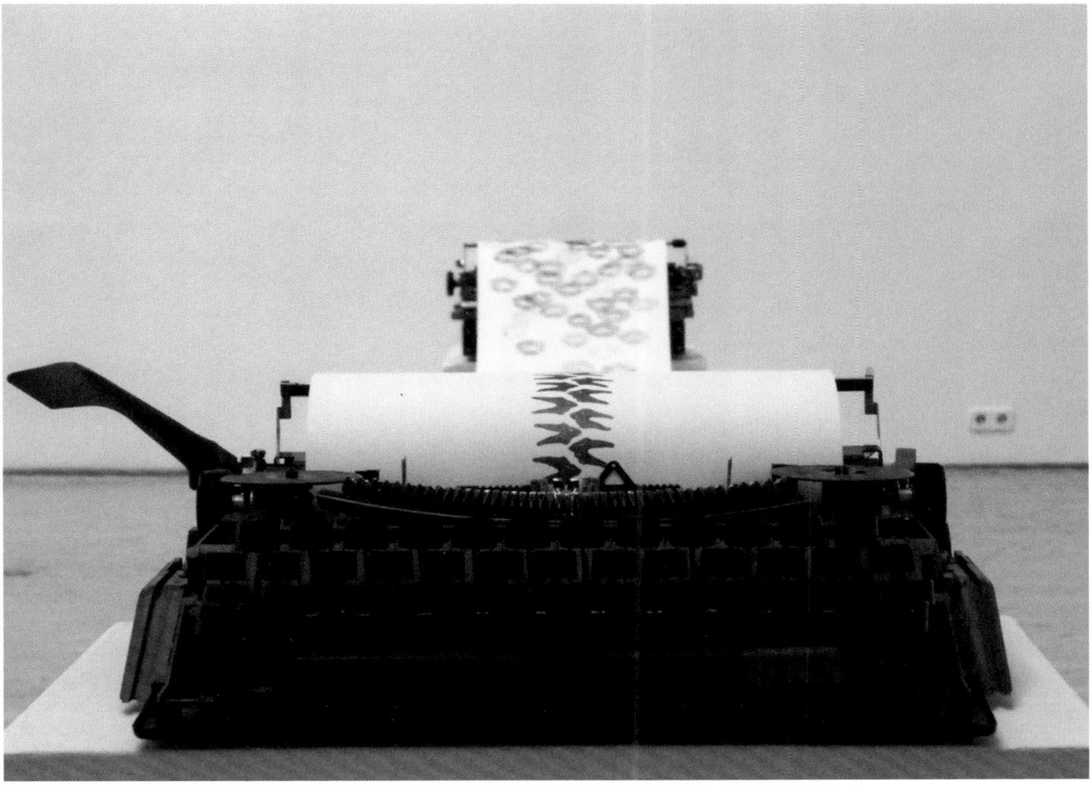

SELF AWARENESS

AT SIMON GORITSCHNIG

Installation with scaffolding, ink-jet printer and prints

50

SELF AWARENESS is an installation that consists mainly of a steel framework and an ink-jet printing device. The printer is "caught" inside the construction, hanging in the air. Although the position might seem quite uncomfortable, it is still printing. Prints, copies and also sketches and drawings can be seen, lying on the ground. All of them show similar images: the printer prints its own building blocks, and thus every piece of paper depicts another part of the device.

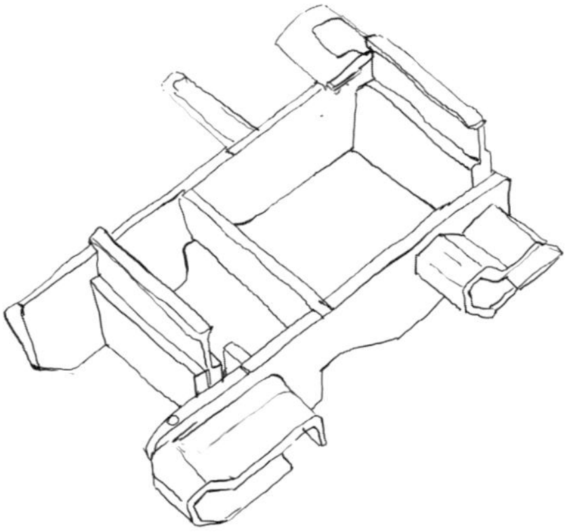

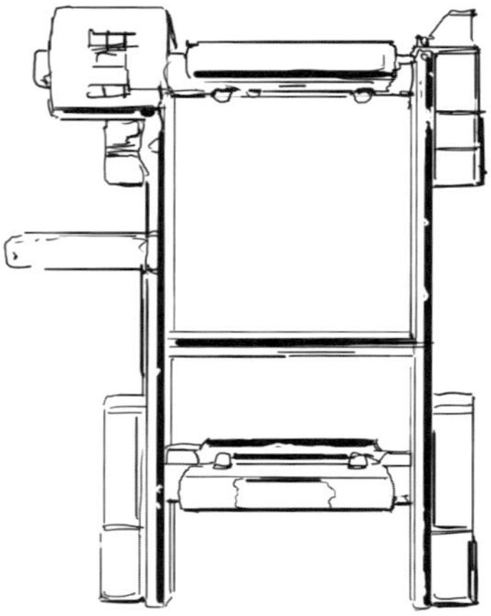

It is the nature of our lives as human beings that we are able to ask questions that we cannot answer: even in a moment in which one might think one knows everything about oneself, one has already changed.

This is the paradox of introspection.

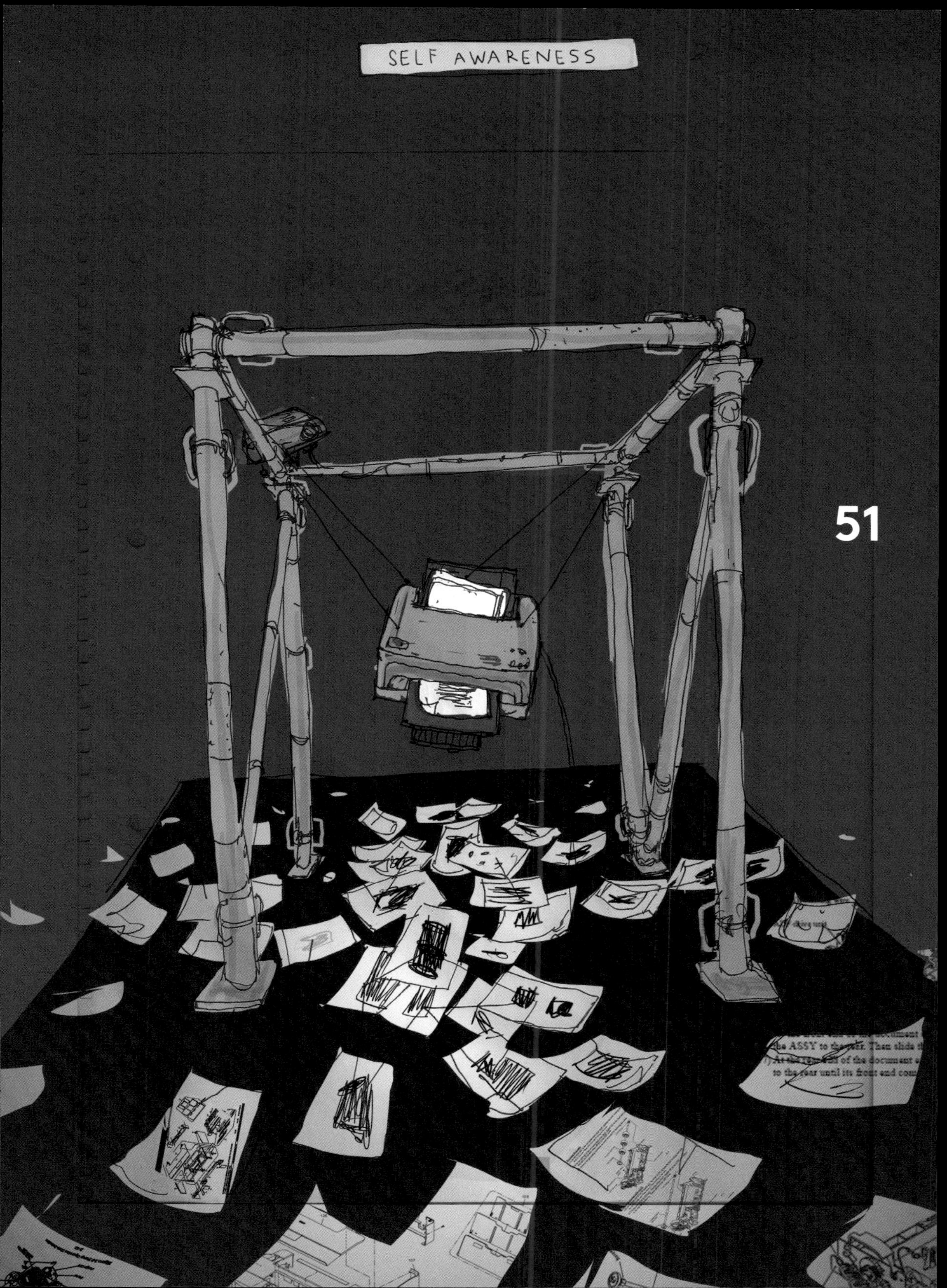
SELF AWARENESS

RED IS THE FUTURE

DE JULIAN IRLINGER

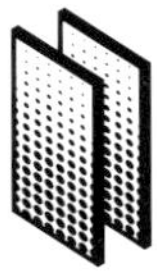

Silkscreens on plexiglas (laid on paper)

GREEN IS THE PAST

+ CRIMINAL SURFACE

52

red is the future green is the past: Permanently separated areas are paradoxically related; due to successive contrast, one colour inevitably refers to its contrasting colour.

In my imagination, a similar connection exists between levels of time which appear apart from each other. For instance, those influencing ideologies and aesthetics. *criminal surface* refers to Adolf Loos' text "Ornament und Verbrechen" (1908). Loos is considered to be one of the founders of modern architecture and puristic aesthetics. This theory and practice generated parameters which influenced the development of the white cube, and hence have shaped exhibition situations until the present. Loos' buildings are located in the vicinity of the exhibition spaces.

My interest lies in the opposition between the convictions of the architecture of the Heiligenkreuzerhof and the modernistic form of the floor sculptures.

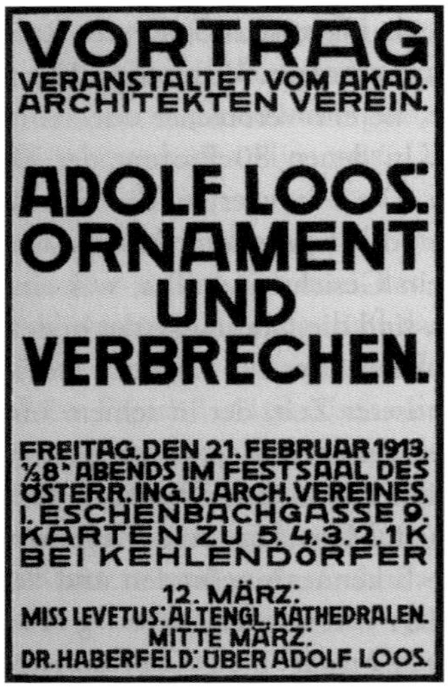

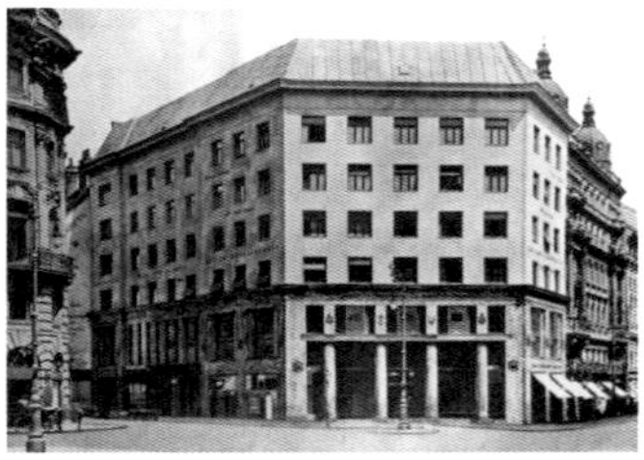

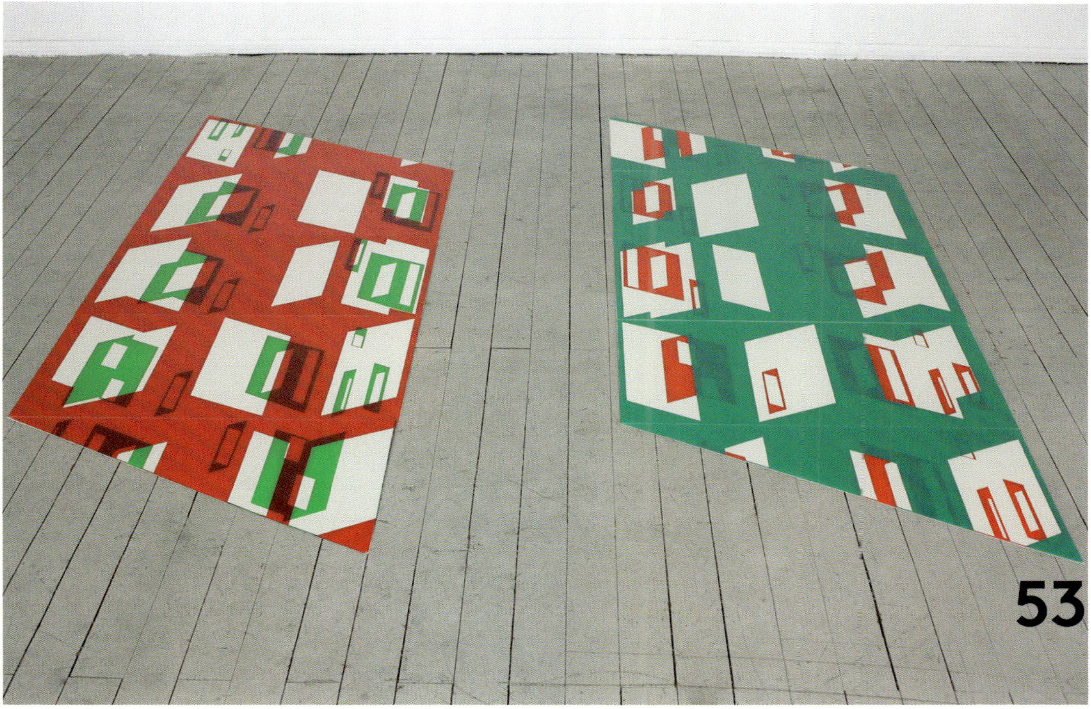

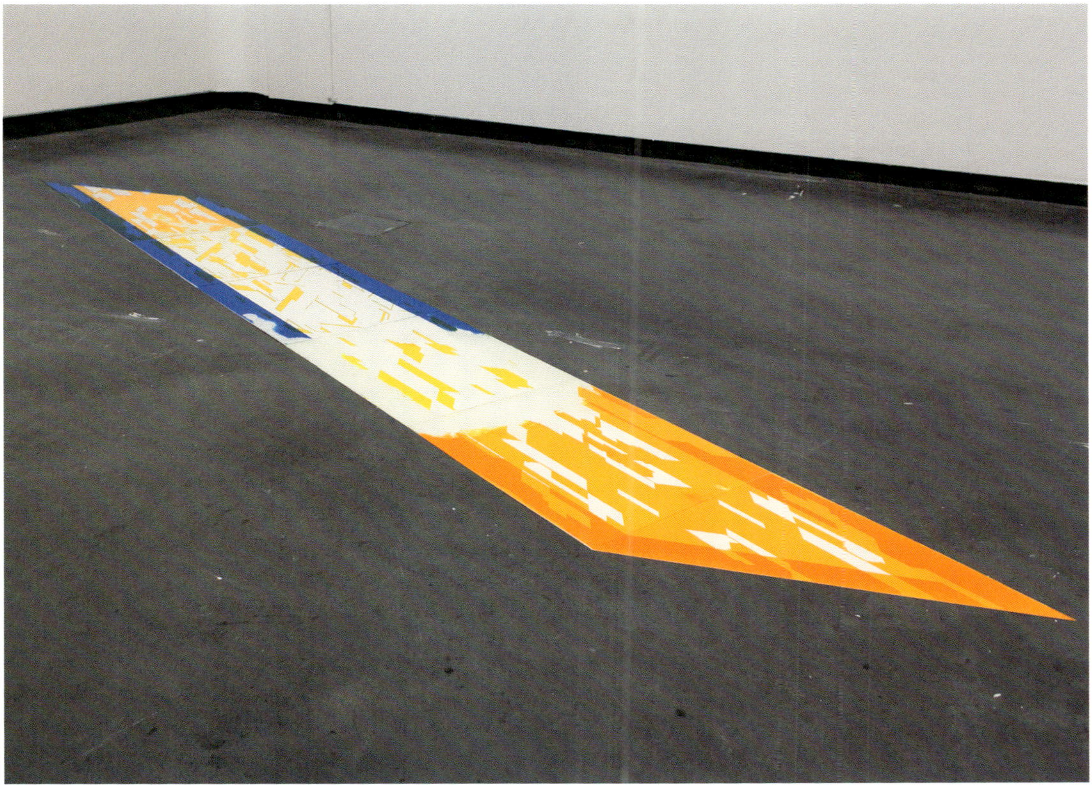

ALTGR + 5°

HU KATA MORAVSZKI
PÉTER ÜVEGES

Video

54

This gif video looks a lot like those video games we remember from our childhood: old-timer animations full of pixels like Mario or bloody shooting games. It was important to use gif technology so that still pictures could be animated as well. Film sequences and still images alternate, creating the action together. In the video’s audio track we wanted to recall several musical atmospheres, among them the 8-bit sounds of the elementary video games of the 90s. Today there is a subcultural kinship between those sounds and gif video.

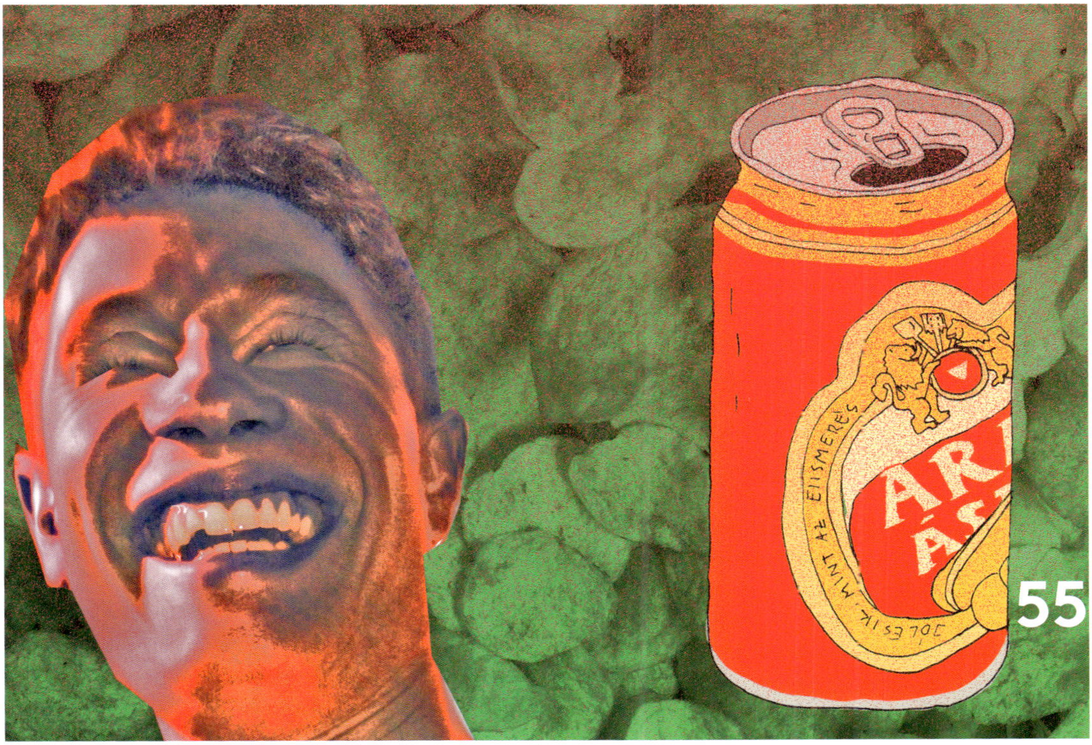
JÓLESIK, MINT AZ ELISMERÉS

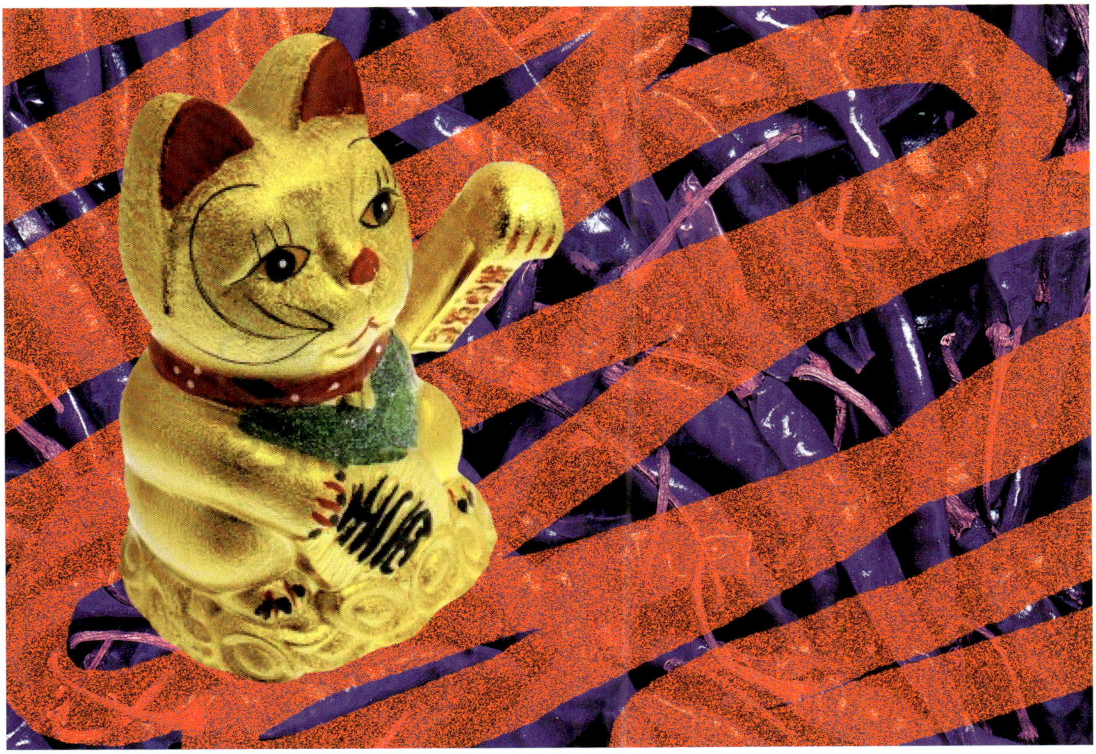

ALL OF MY WASTED BRILLIANT IDEAS

AT XENIA OSTROVSKAYA

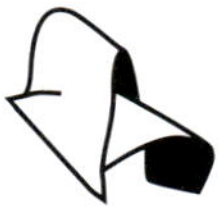

Installation with
porcelain paper objects

56

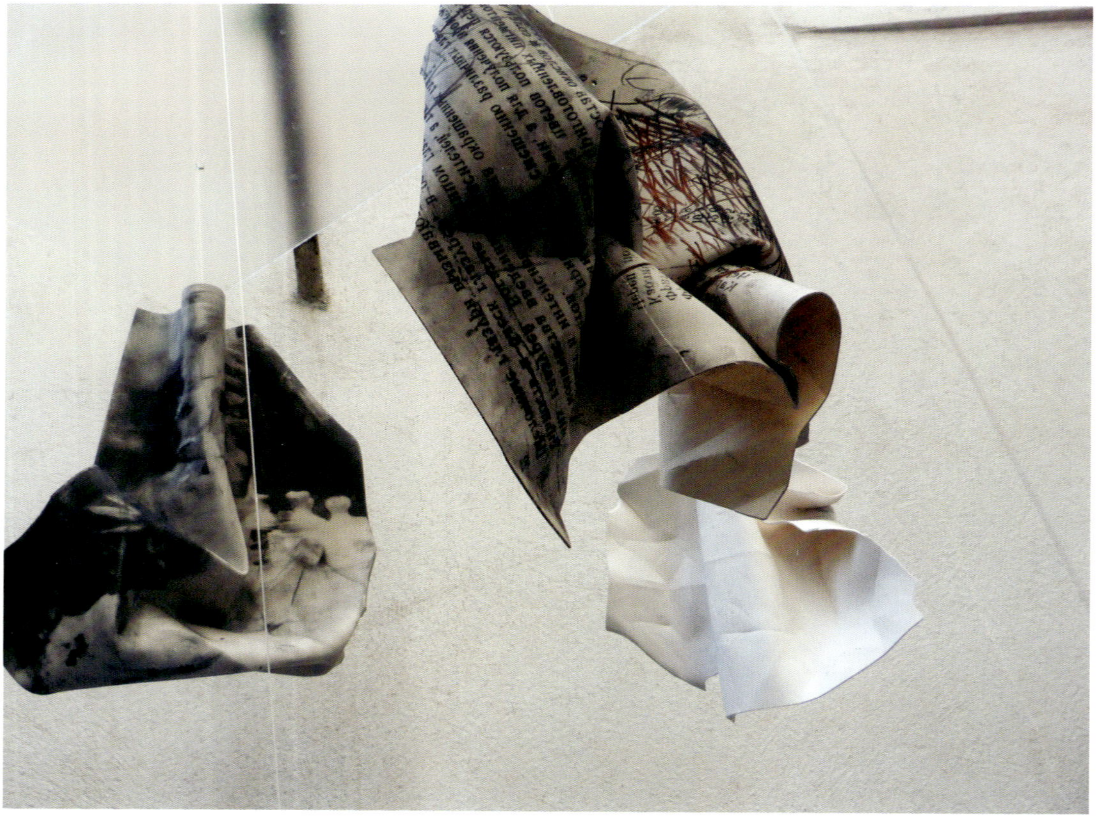

Among all the ways of finding the best solution for a problem, I always choose brainstorming. I let the most absurd ideas rush through my head and wait for the one that can later be developed into the right thing. All the others are usually rejected for some reason. Hence the overall result is that tons of sketches end up in the rubbish bin. Sometimes I wonder what makes me find one idea better than the other. Am I not mistaken? Who knows, maybe it was just yesterday that I threw away the most brilliant idea I ever had. This is something I'll never know.

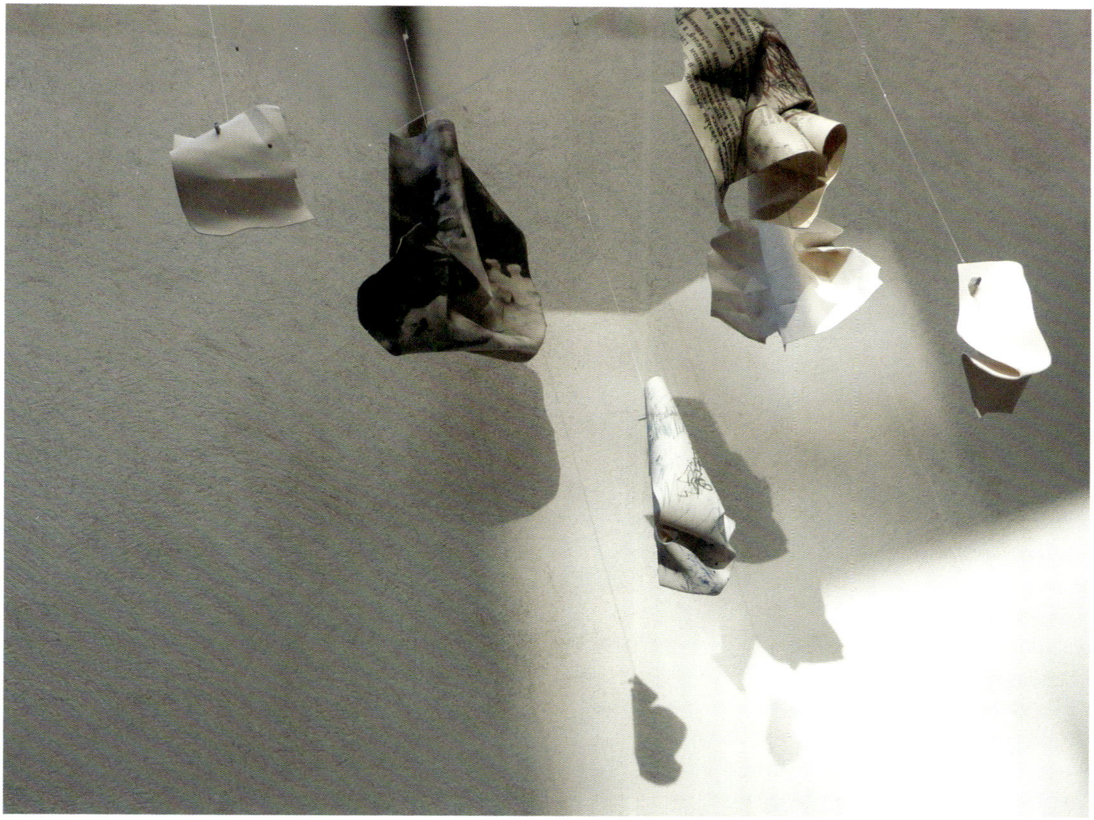

SCHNEE

GB HANS-JÖRG POCHMANN

Linocut

58

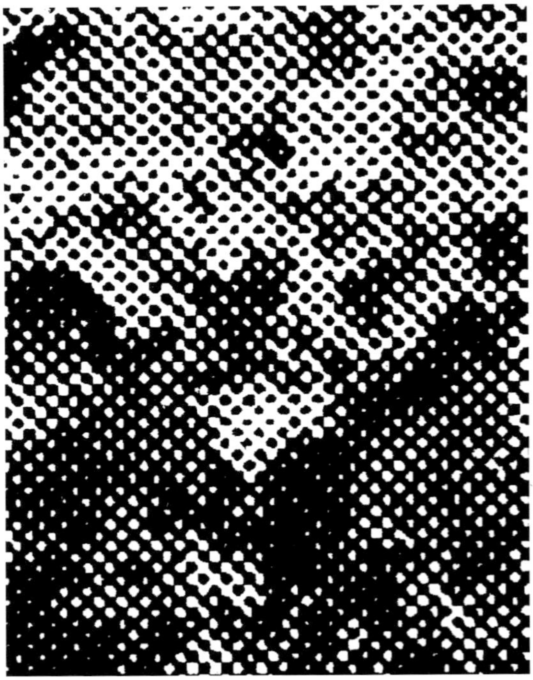

here is the snow | here is the dirt / _ here is the digital photograph here is the light
| here is the light sensor | here is the electric charge _ here is the laser print of the
photograph here is the toner | here is the paper _ here is the scan of the laser print
here is the light | here is the reflection | here is the light sensor | here is the electric
charge | here may be the magnetic charge _ here is the enlarged laser print of the
scan here is the toner | here is the paper _ here is the acetone | here is the lino-
leum | here is the knife | here is the ink | here is the paper / _ here are letters here is
the other ink | here is the other paper / _ here are you.

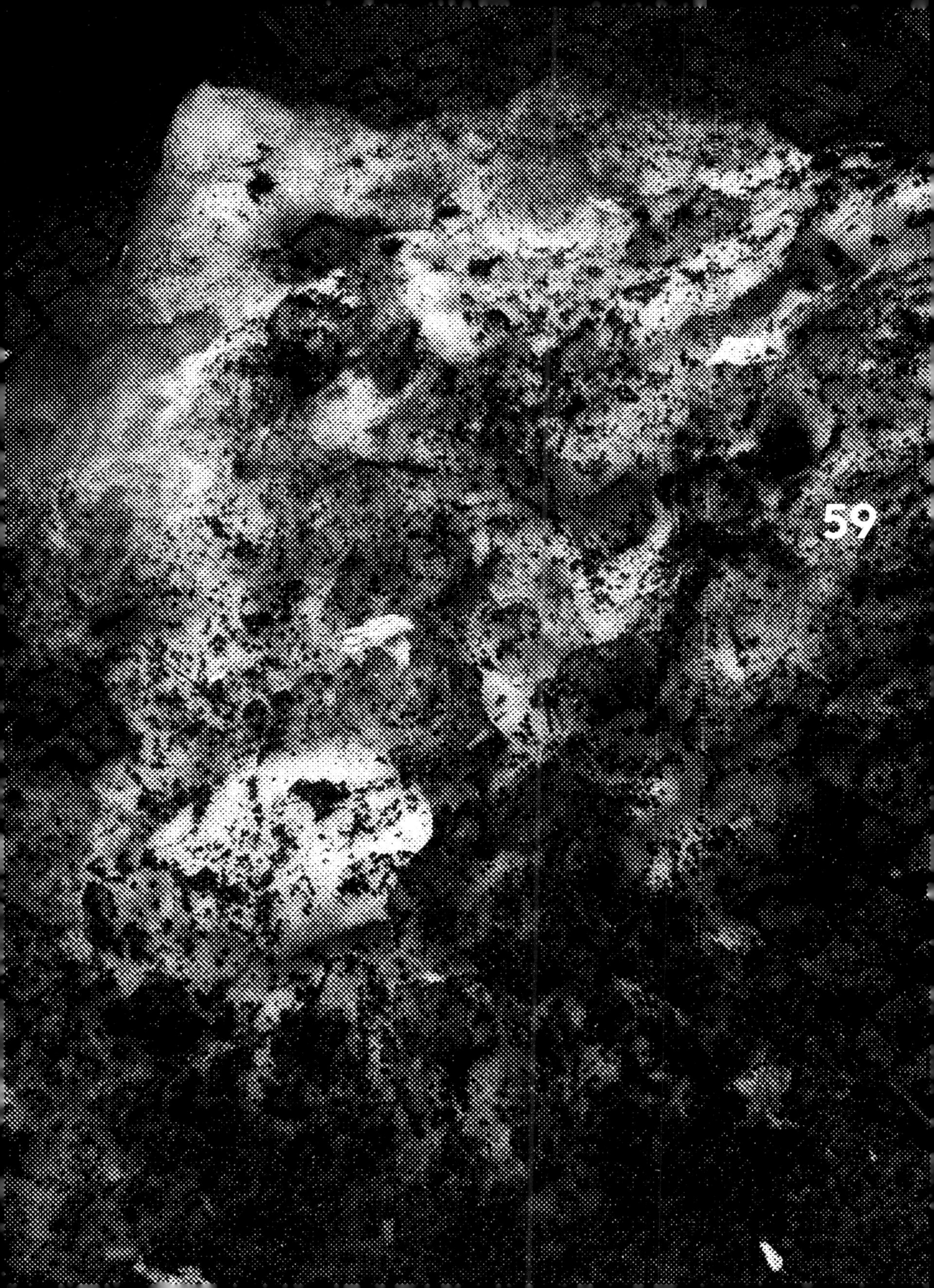

VIEWS AND PROSPECTS

DE PHILIP POPPEK

Poster distribution project

60

FROM A TOURISTIC TRIP WITH A MORE OR LESS POLITICAL BACKGROUND (FOR TAKE-AWAY)

All images were taken in summer 2012 on a journey from Belgrade, Serbia to Priština, Kosovo. If you like the posters, feel free to grab one of them, take it home and hang it where it fits in best with your flat décor: kitchen, floor, bathroom or over the bed.

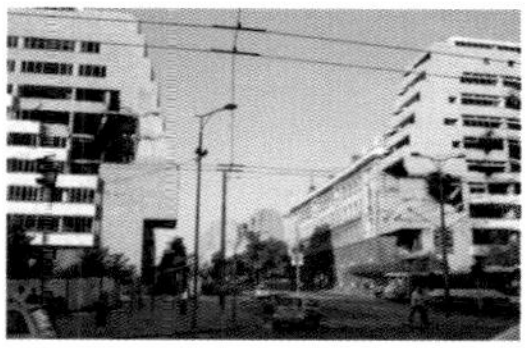

views

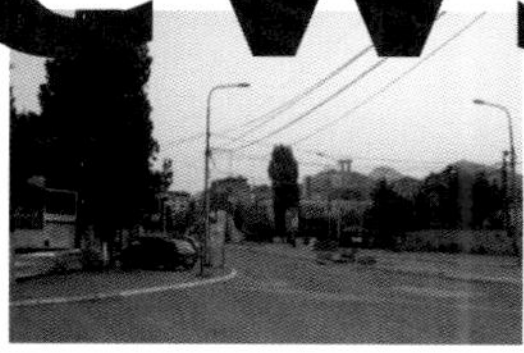

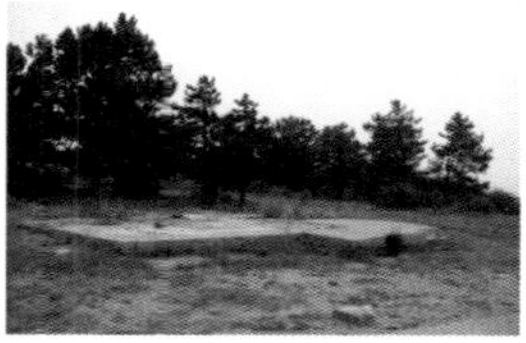

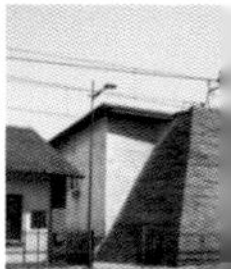

backg

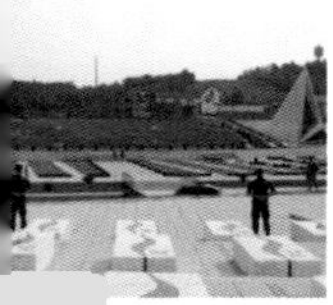

from

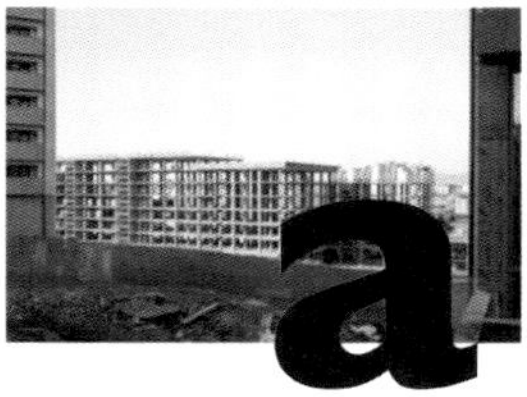

a to

b

ADDENDUM SKY

MEG RAHAIM

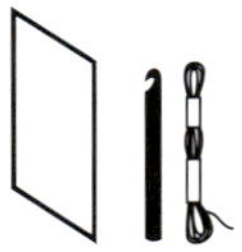

crocheted yarn

62

Lines 113 and 114 with revisions

113 (121) (150.04)

31 30 30 30

BBBBBBBBBBBBBWBBBWBBBBBBBBBWBWW
BWWWBWBWWBBBBWWBWBBBBBBBBBBBBB
WBBBBWBBBBBBBWBBWBWBWWBWWBWWWB
WWBWWBWWWWWWBWWWWBWWWWWWWWWWWW

(151) 30 30 30 30 31

BBBBBBBBBBBWBBBWBBWBBBWBBBBBWB
BBWBWWWBWWWWWWBWWWWBWBWBWWWBWB
BBBBBBBWBWBWBWBWBWBBWBBWWBWBWB
BBWBBWWWBWWBWWBWWWWWWWWBWWWWWW
WWWWWWWWWWWWWWWWWWWWWWWWWWWWWWW

114 (121) (150.04)

31 30 30 30

BBBBBBBBBWBBBBBBWBBBBBBWBBBWBWW
BWWWWWWBWBBBWBBWBBBBBBBWBBWBBW
BBWBBWBWBBBBBBWBWBWWBWBWWBWWWW
BWWBWWWWWWWWBWWWWWBWWWWWWWWWWW

(151) 30 30 30 30 31

BBBBBBBBBWBBBWBBBBWBBWBBBBBWBW
WBBWBWWBWWWWWWWWWBWWBWBBWBWBBB
BWBBWBBWBWBWWBWBWBBWBBWBWBBBBB
BBBWBWBWWBWBWWWWWWWWWWBWWBWWWW
BWWWWWWBWWWWWWWBWWWWWWWWWWWWWWW

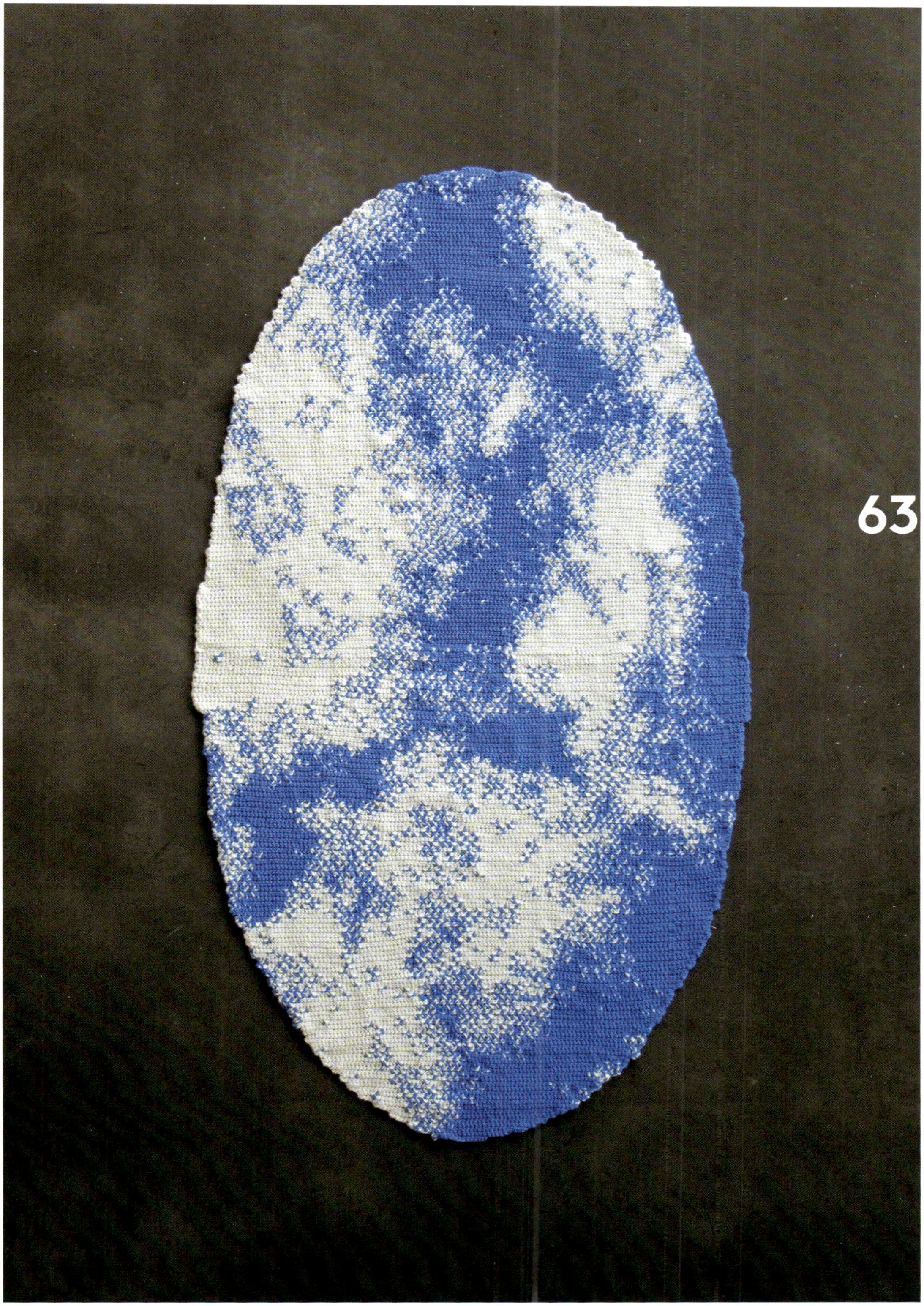

BLANK

DE ROBERT SCHWARK

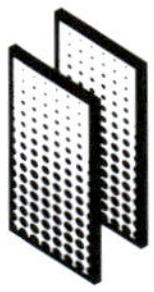

Aluminum printing plates on panel

64

The medium of printmaking is the technical origin of our mass-media interfaces. Günther Anders understands printmaking as a characteristic aspect of consumer society and sees the mass media as a kind of printing block. The beholder becomes the imprint of a mass-media matrix.

1 After being printed, the printing block recedes into the background. It is forgotten. But it remains a form of memory and a pattern of the prints. The printing block can be described as "the original".

2 The series Blank comprises 15 printing blocks mounted on an aluminium panel. The individual images question the intellectual heritage and the character of our imagination/perception. The panel as a whole functions as a matrix. As a manual pattern that turns the beholder into a screen and imprints him/her.

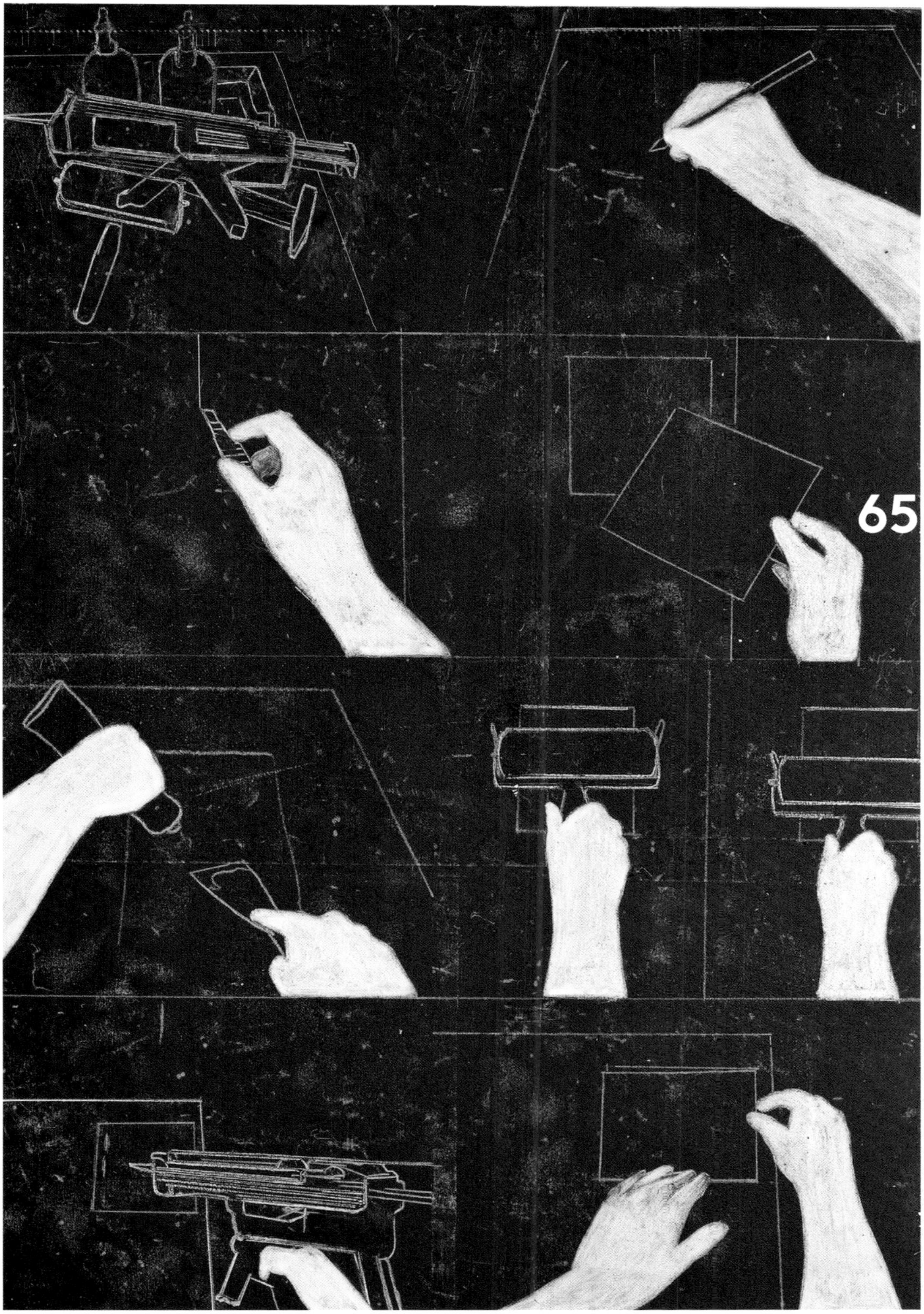

GARDEN

HU LÍDIA TAKÁCS

Lithographs

66

My work consists of nine lithographs in three sizes, whereby the starting point for each picture is an image from a garden. Each of the lithographs includes a hidden symbol that becomes more and more visible with the reduction of size.

For me the most interesting part of printmaking is the influence of the materials. One can always spot small differences while comparing the original to the final print. The scaling of the prints was important: I had to repeat the printing faults of the largest pictures, which were made first. In this way, I was forced to face both my own and the machines' mistakes. The alterations caused by the materials stratified in two layers on the smallest prints. They symbolize the confrontation with the impossibility of perfection.

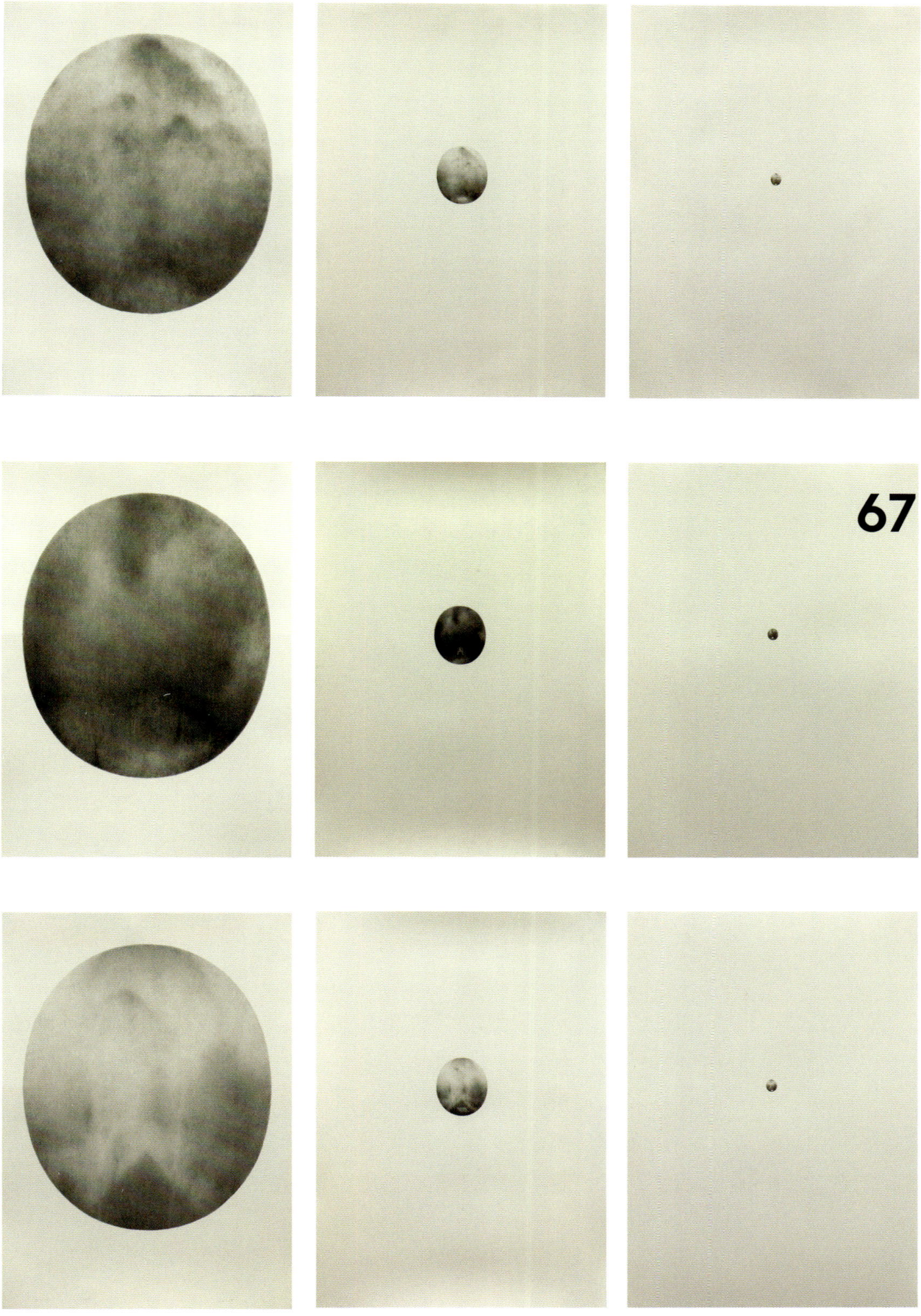

GUARDING THE BOARDERS

SK PAVOL TRUBEN

Installation with boat skeleton and travel applications

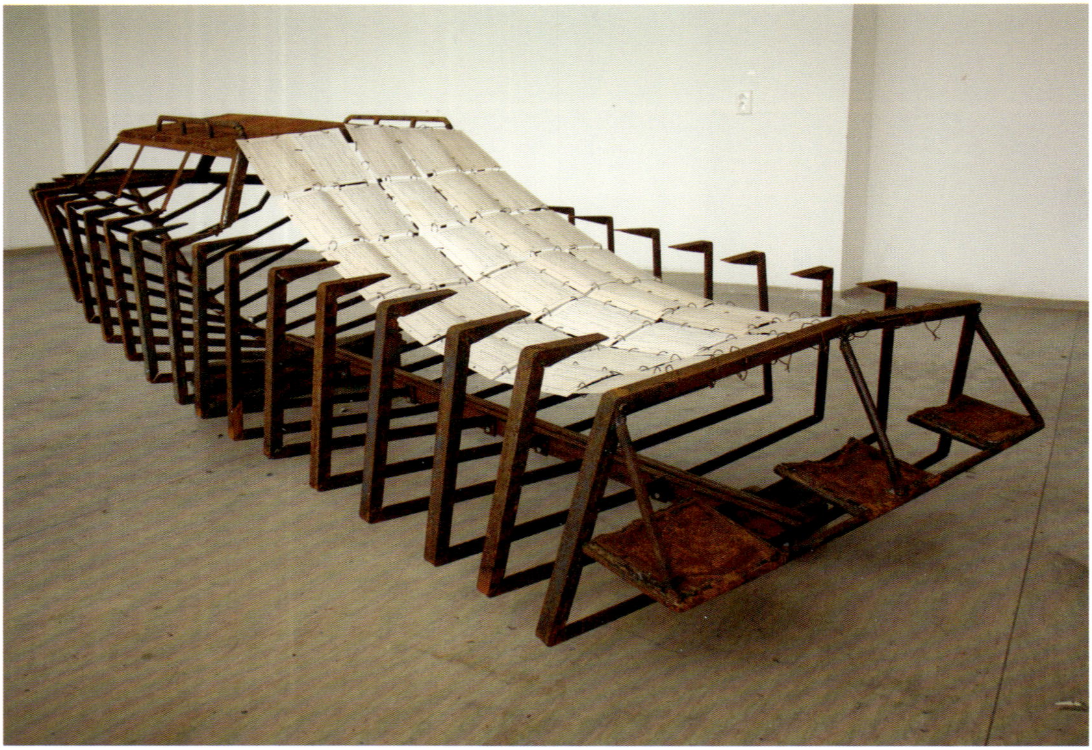

The object is inspired by the boat Volvo Penta GSB 066. This model was used to guard the border river under Communism. Its rusted skeleton is a reminder of the Slovak-Austrian border, which was a contact point of East and West. At least 42 people were killed in cold blood in 1948–1949 while attempting to illegally cross this border.

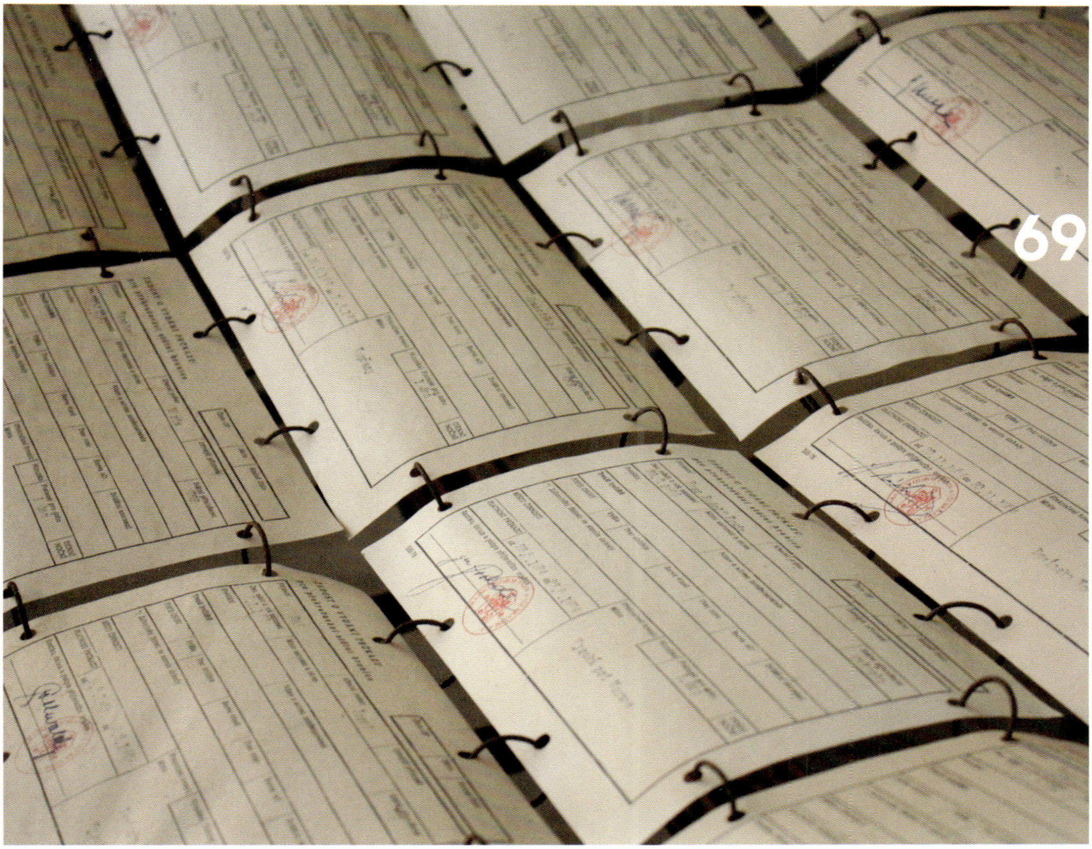

Exactly the same number (42) of applications to cross the border legally are attached to the object. Slovakia has not yet been able to assign criminal responsibility for these "murders" under Communism. Thus this object, by its form, recalls the skeleton in the closet that we as a country are failing to deal with.

HYDROGEN

HU RÉKA VIDRA

Mezzotints in
Petri dishes

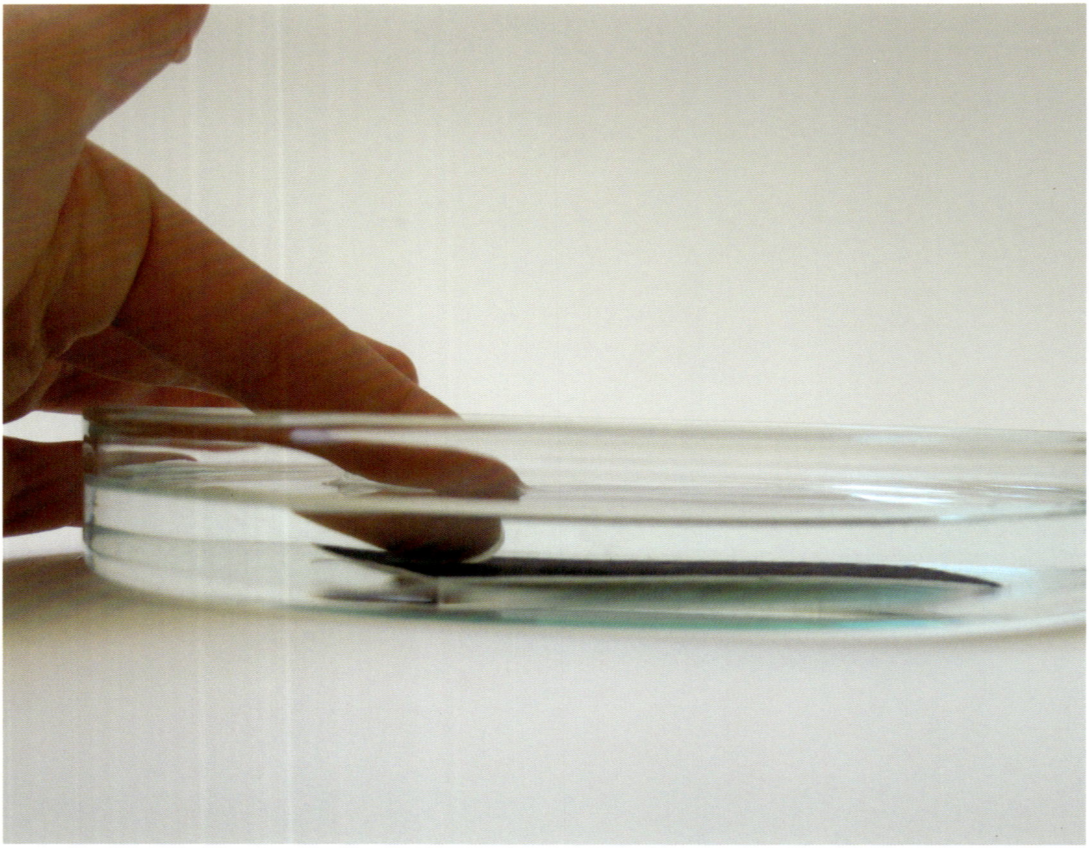

do I have dimensions beyond the valence electrons
or do I exist inside the nucleus again?
because nowadays thoughts are not born,
they only conceive,
the fertilized cell resigns and
leaves.

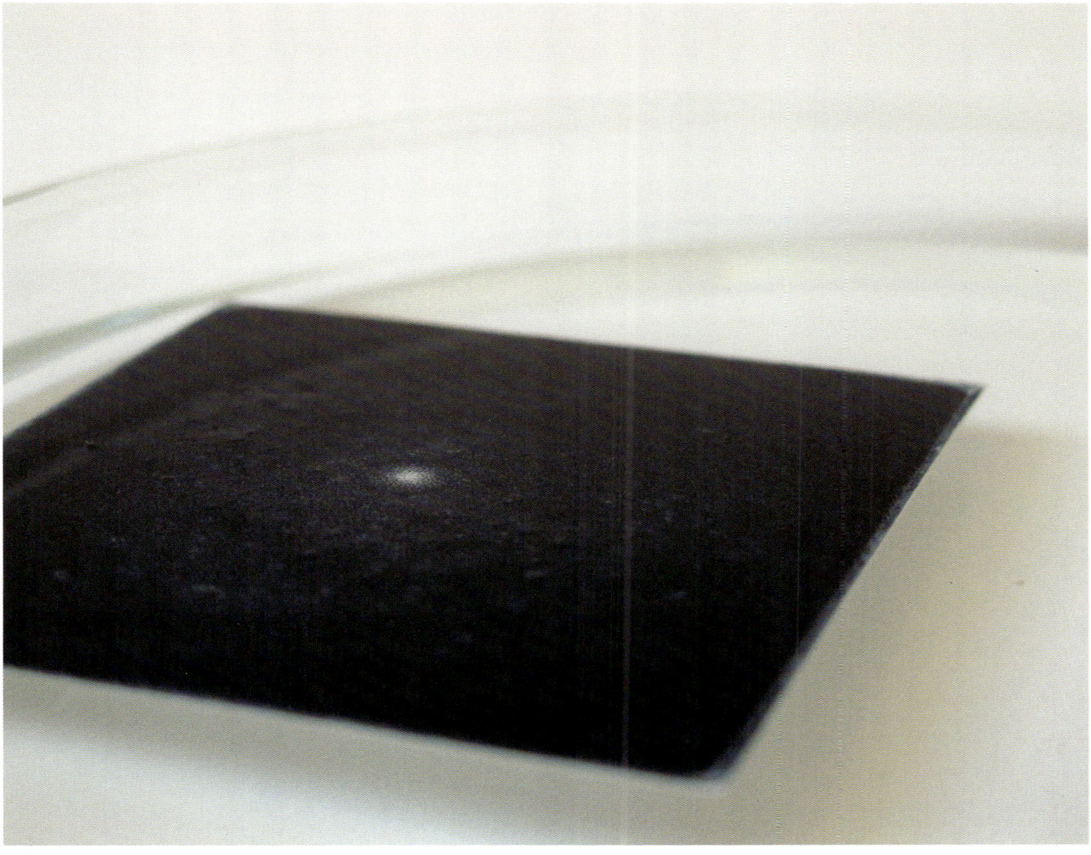

SPEAK TO THE EYE

GB SHARON WHYTE

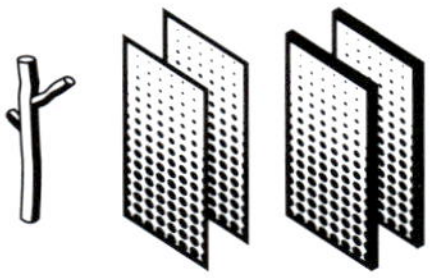

Installation, wood construction with digital print and screen print on paper

72

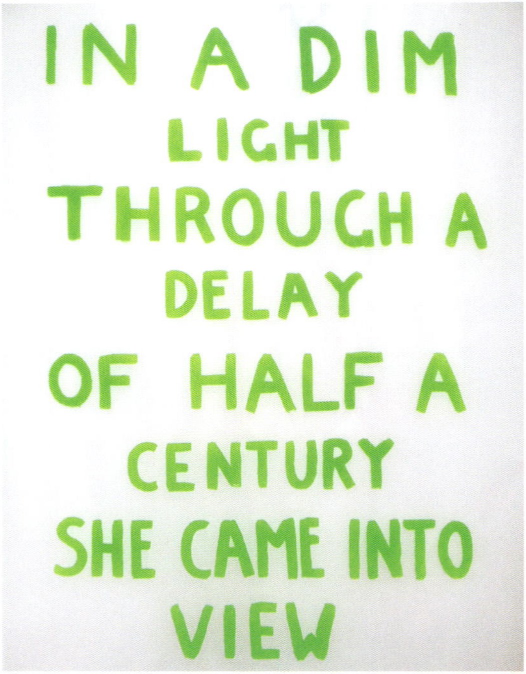

To become an image, the performance must take place. The tools of the performer become the tools of the artist. The performer becomes the tool of the artist. The machine: two sides of a story. The interior does not conform with the exterior. The interior thoughts are of a nature that cannot be explained in the language of the poster, the external voice of the machine. It spits out a garbled message. The inner world has ceased to be part of this game: having fallen in love with its own narrative, it reflects further and further in on itself. It has become finite, its own archive, transforming nothing. The viewer: the central figure, but also the outside observer – both positions that the artistic process demands.

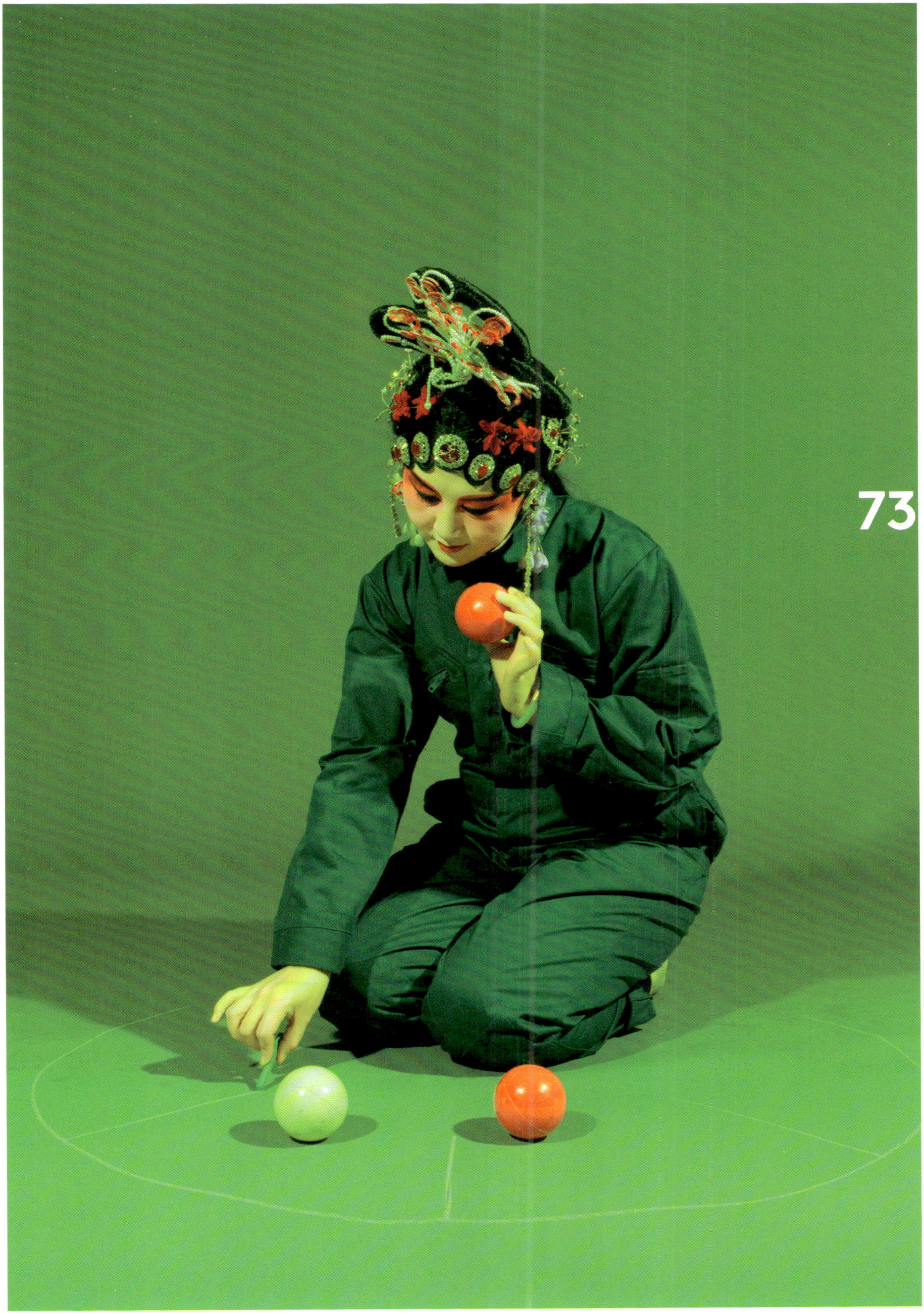

SPACE-SWING

DE **SUSAN WINTER**

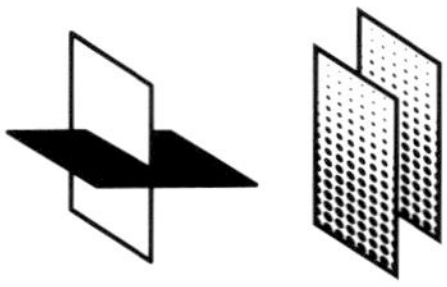

Mixed media installation

74

How could the idea of a space-swing be represented? Hanging from a satellite, a swing moves freely above the earth. The astronomic dimensions involved make it impossible to exhibit a nylon thread of suitable length. But wound into a ball and scaled down, the thread evokes a yet undiscovered planet. It seems necessary to retreat to an image: a swing of earthly dimensions, which due to its lightness seems to hover, nevertheless embodies the dream of flying. Being made from white feathers, it exaggerates the dream of flying through its over-stylization, and the swing itself seems to float. The white colour of the feathers refers to a moment of "less-ness" from the earthly, but also to the infinite cosmos, or, as it is put in Moby Dick:

»Is it that by its indefiniteness it shadows forth the heartless voids and immensities of the universe, and thus stabs us from behind with the thought of annihilation [...]?«

Herman Melville, Moby Dick,
chapter 42: The Whiteness of the Whale.

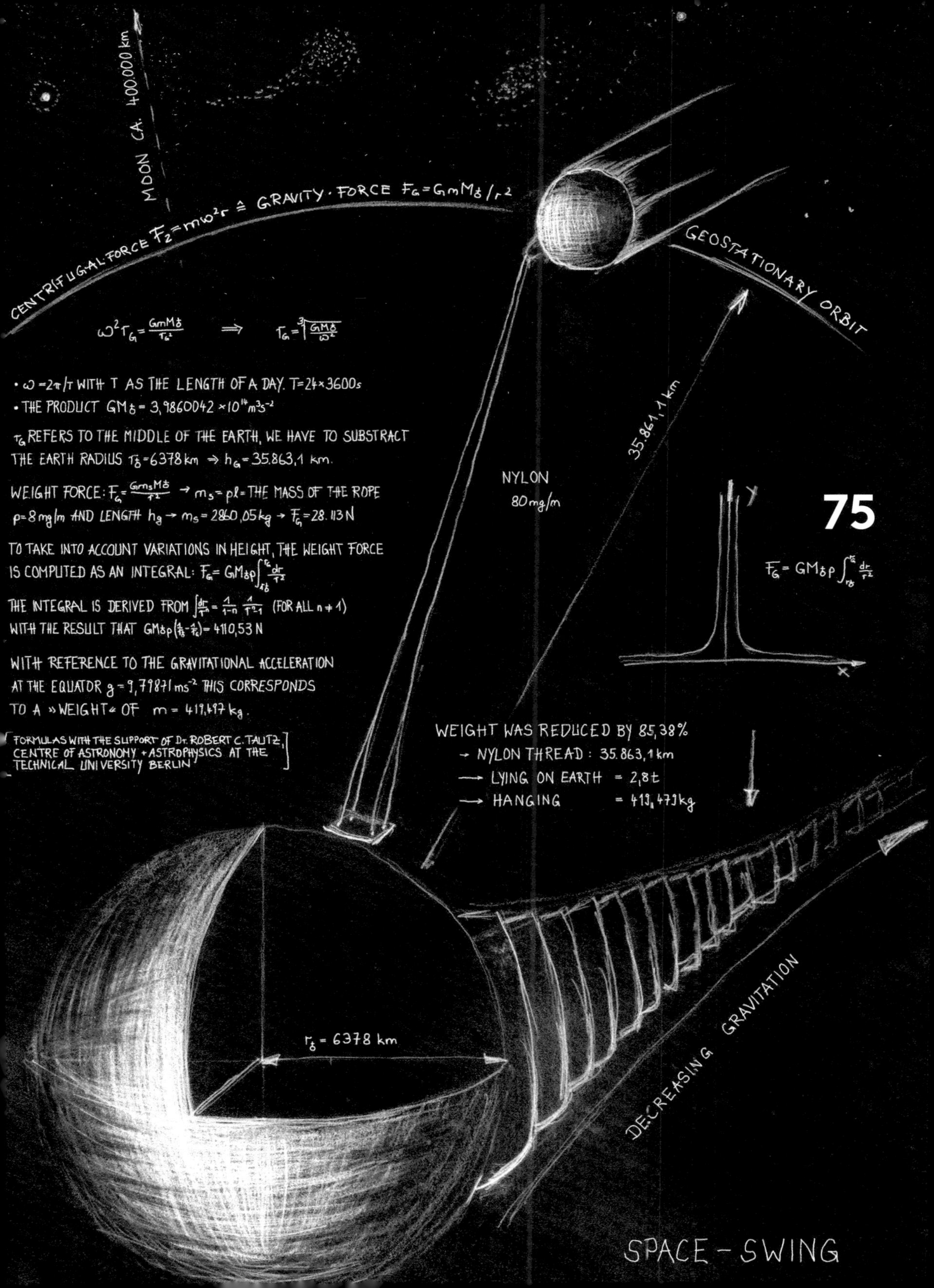
MOON CA. 400.000 km
CENTRIFUGAL FORCE $F_Z = m\omega^2 r \triangleq$ GRAVITY · FORCE $F_G = GmM_♁/r^2$
GEOSTATIONARY ORBIT
$\omega^2 r_G = \frac{GmM_♁}{r_G^2} \Longrightarrow r_G = \sqrt[3]{\frac{GM_♁}{\omega^2}}$
• $\omega = 2\pi/T$ WITH T AS THE LENGTH OF A DAY. $T = 24 \times 3600s$
• THE PRODUCT $GM_♁ = 3{,}9860042 \times 10^{14} m^3 s^{-2}$
r_G REFERS TO THE MIDDLE OF THE EARTH, WE HAVE TO SUBSTRACT
THE EARTH RADIUS $r_♁ = 6378$ km $\Rightarrow h_G = 35.863{,}1$ km.
WEIGHT FORCE: $F_G = \frac{Gm_s M_♁}{r^2} \rightarrow m_s = \rho l =$ THE MASS OF THE ROPE
$\rho = 8$ mg/m AND LENGTH $h_g \rightarrow m_s = 2860{,}05$ kg $\rightarrow F_G = 28.113$ N
TO TAKE INTO ACCOUNT VARIATIONS IN HEIGHT, THE WEIGHT FORCE
IS COMPUTED AS AN INTEGRAL: $F_G = GM_♁\rho \int_{r_♁}^{r_G} \frac{dr}{r^2}$
THE INTEGRAL IS DERIVED FROM $\int \frac{dr}{r^n} = \frac{1}{1-n} \frac{1}{r^{n-1}}$ (FOR ALL $n \neq 1$)
WITH THE RESULT THAT $GM_♁\rho\left(\frac{1}{r_♁} - \frac{1}{r_G}\right) = 4110{,}53$ N
WITH REFERENCE TO THE GRAVITATIONAL ACCELERATION
AT THE EQUATOR $g = 9{,}79871 ms^{-2}$ THIS CORRESPONDS
TO A »WEIGHT« OF $m = 419{,}497$ kg.
FORMULAS WITH THE SUPPORT OF Dr. ROBERT C. TAUTZ,
CENTRE OF ASTRONOMY + ASTROPHYSICS AT THE
TECHNICAL UNIVERSITY BERLIN
NYLON
80 mg/m
35.861,1 km
y
x
$F_G = GM_♁\rho \int_{r_♁}^{r_G} \frac{dr}{r^2}$
WEIGHT WAS REDUCED BY 85,38%
→ NYLON THREAD : 35.863,1 km
→ LYING ON EARTH = 2,8 t
→ HANGING = 419,479 kg
$r_♁ = 6378$ km
DECREASING GRAVITATION
SPACE – SWING

IMPRINT

Jan Svenungsson,
Department for Graphics and Printmaking,
University of Applied Arts Vienna, Austria

AMBRA | V is part of
Medecco Holding GmbH, Vienna
Printed in Austria

Photographs and illustrations:
all photographs and reproductions of work were made by the respective artists themselves, except: p.40-41 photo: Marko Göhre, courtesy Galerie M2A, Dresden; p.45 photo: Katharina Reckendorfer; p.52 (poster) colour lithograph by Adolf Loos, printed by A. Berger, Vienna 1913; p.52 (building) Looshaus August 1910, wienwiki.net; p.65 photo: Jens Klein; p.67 photo: János Barta

Graphic design, pictograms and word images:
Theresa Hattinger
Copy editing: Christopher Barber
Edited by Jan Svenungsson,
assisted by Larissa Leverenz
Printing: Holzhausen Druck GmbH, A-Wolkersdorf

Printed on acid-free and chlorine-free bleached paper

With 53 colored figures

ISSN1866-248X
ISBN 978-3-99043-623-3